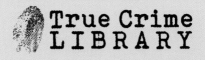

MODERN-DAY PIRATES

**DRUG CARTELS AND SMUGGLERS
INFAMOUS TERRORISTS
MASS MURDERERS
MODERN-DAY PIRATES
ORGANIZED CRIME
SERIAL KILLERS**

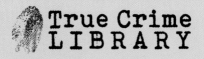
True Crime
LIBRARY

MODERN-DAY PIRATES

LeeAnne Gelletly

ELDORADO INK

Eldorado Ink
PO Box 100097
Pittsburgh, PA 15233
www.eldoradoink.com

Produced by OTTN Publishing, Stockton, New Jersey

CPSIA compliance information: Batch#CS2013-4. For further information,
contact Eldorado Ink at info@eldoradoink.com.

First printing

1 3 5 7 9 8 6 4 2

Library of Congress Cataloging-in-Publication Data
available from the Library of Congress

ISBN-13: 978-1-61900-037-7 (hc)
ISBN-13: 978-1-61900-038-4 (trade)
ISBN-13: 978-1-61900-039-1 (ebook)

*For information about custom editions, special sales, or premiums,
please contact our special sales department at info@eldoradoink.com.*

TABLE OF CONTENTS

Somali pirates armed with AK-47 rifles keep watch on the coastline at Hobyo, a town in northeastern Somalia that is a notorious pirate base.

MODERN PIRACY
AN INTRODUCTION

Maritime piracy—attacks on both the high seas and territorial waters—has existed since the first sailors set to sea. The practice of robbery and kidnapping continues today as armed, well-equipped modern-day pirates attack vessels around the world.

The International Maritime Bureau (IMB), a division of the International Chamber of Commerce (ICC), defines modern piracy as:

> An act of boarding or attempting to board any ship anywhere with the apparent intent to commit theft or any other crime and with the apparent intent or capability to use force in the furtherance of that act.

During the 1990s and early 2000s the issue of piracy was a serious problem in the waters of Southeast Asia, especially around Indonesia. The hotspot was the Straits of Malacca, part of an important sea route between China and India. The 550-mile-long strait connects the Indian Ocean with the South China Sea and the Pacific Ocean. An estimated 40 percent of the world's annual trade passes through the Straits of Malacca. Each year about 50,000 vessels travel through sea lanes adjacent to the nations of Indonesia (notably the island of Sumatra) and Malaysia. By 2000, more than half the number of pirate attacks reported each year were occurring in the Straits of Malacca. Pirate activity was also fairly common in the waters around Bangladesh, India, Indonesia, Malaysia, and Vietnam, as well as in the South China Sea.

Pirates operating in Southeast Asia seized mostly small tankers, tugs, and barges. Their goals varied from robbing crews to taking cargos to stealing ships. They had little regard for captured

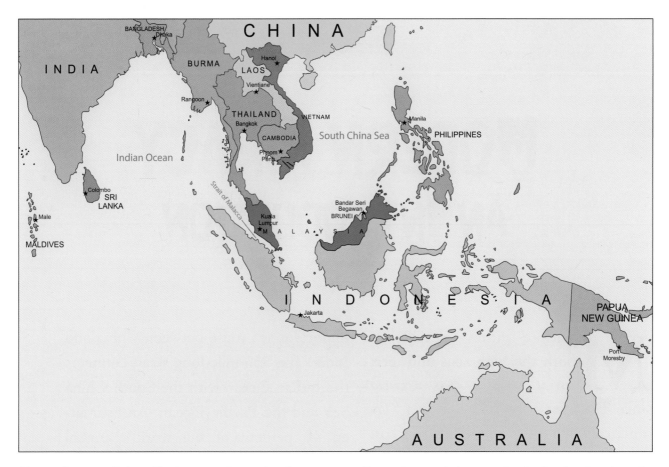

Piracy has traditionally been a threat in the waters of southeast Asia, particularly the Straits of Malacca between Indonesia, Malaysia, and Singapore.

crews, who were at risk of being injured, killed, or set adrift.

By the early years of the 21st century, there were increasing reports of pirate activity along the coast of east Africa. This area is known as the "Horn of Africa," and is adjacent to an important shipping waterway, the Gulf of Aden.

Named after the Yemeni port city of Aden, the Gulf of Aden borders Yemen to the north and Somalia to the south. Somalia is an example of a "failed state"—a country where there is no legitimate government and various armed factions struggle for power. In this lawless environment, pirates could flourish. It didn't help that Somalia is one of the world's poorest countries, making piracy an appealing job for unemployed young men. Somali pirates soon began targeting vessels in the Gulf of Aden.

The Gulf is one of the world's busiest shipping lanes, part of a major sea route connecting Europe, the Middle East, and Asia. Each year more than 20,000 commercial ships pass through the gulf—including oil tankers that carry an estimated 10 percent of the world's crude oil. Other commercial ships carry goods to and from the Mediterranean Sea in Europe via the Suez Canal.

In the late 1990s Somali pirates began charging "fees" from commercial ships that they stopped because they were in Somali waters. By the mid-2000s Somali pirates were seizing ships and their crews, and refusing to release them until they received huge ransom payments. By 2007 Somali piracy was considered a major problem.

At the same time the western coast of Africa, particularly the Gulf of Guinea, was also plagued by pirate attacks. Indonesian and Somali pirates were mostly responsible for hijackings at sea, while Nigerian pirates struck more often in territorial waters (defined as 12 nautical miles from the coast) off Nigeria, Ghana, and the Ivory Coast. Typical attacks involved stealing from ships while they were in the harbor or anchored offshore. Nigerian pirates

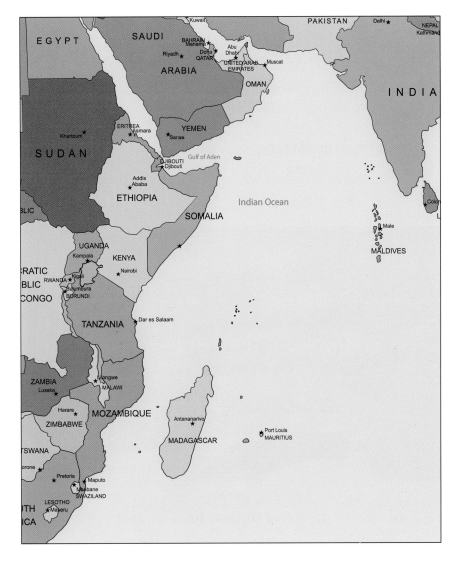

This map of east Africa, the Arabian Peninsula, and central Asia shows the Gulf of Aden and the Indian Ocean, where Somali pirates have been operating with near-impunity since the late 1990s.

often seized ships for their cargos of gasoline and sometimes kidnapped crew members.

The IMB has identified the coastlines of Brazil, Peru, and Venezuela as regions in South America with serious problems of piracy and armed robbery. In most cases, pirates attack vessels while they are in port. For example, in the Puerto la Cruz area of Venezuela bandits are known to attack boats at night. They pull small fishing boats up to vessels that are at anchor, and in the darkness climb aboard. They gag, use knives and guns to threaten and beat the crew, seeking cargo, money, and other valuables. Cases are typically dealt with by local police or port authorities.

METHOD OF ATTACK

Ships are hijacked when they are boarded from another ship by pirates. In

Rocket-propelled grenades (RPGs) and the clip from an AK-47 rifle, seized from pirates operating in the Indian Ocean.

some cases crew members or passengers on the ship may be the people behind an attack. However, such "inside jobs" are rare. In Somalia, more often gangs of men based in pirate havens—coastal towns that support pirates by providing safe places for them to operate—launch attacks on target vessels.

In a typical raid, several maneuverable high-powered speedboats, usually fiberglass skiffs, are loaded with heavily armed small groups, usually consisting of about 10 pirates. The small boats rapidly approach the target vessel and swarm around it. The pirates gesture to the ship to stop, and threaten it by firing rocket-propelled grenades (RPGs) and machine guns. Once the ship stops the pirates move in, throwing grappling hooks and rope ladders at the stern—where the vessel rides lowest in the water, so they can climb up to the deck. Sometimes, even if a vessel does not stop, a fast skiff can pull even with the ship so pirates can toss their grappling hooks and rope ladders onto the deck in order to board. Hijackers also often board vessels at night, appearing out of the darkness.

Once aboard, pirates typically head for the bridge, the enclosed area from which the captain and officers direct the vessel's operation. This way the pirates can gain control of the steering mechanism. If any crew members try to resist, they will be threatened with a variety of weapons, from machetes to AK-47 rifles. The pirates will often lock up the crew, except for a few key people needed to keep the ship moving in the direction that the pirates want.

When properly planned, pirate attacks can be swift and efficient. It can take as little as 30 minutes for a group of pirates to take control of a ship. Modern merchant ships do not require a large crew, so a dozen well-armed pirates can easily hijack a ship.

TARGETS AND PURPOSE

Pirates have attacked a variety of ships, with the MV (Motor Vessel or Merchant

Vessel) and VLCC (Very Large Crude Carrier, or oil supertanker) among their more popular targets. Other ships that have been targeted by modern-day pirates include cruise ships, passenger ferries, yachts, fishing trawlers, and wooden *dhows*. (The *dhow* is a type of ship with a high-swept bow that is commonly found in the Indian Ocean.)

Pirates often have different motives for capturing various types of ship. For example, when yachts, ferries, or merchant ships are targeted, the pirates may only be interested in robbing those on board. In such cases they search the ship for valuables; take money from the

Cargo ships like MV *Pucon*, pictured above, are often targeted by pirates operating in small boats.

This *dhow* is a pirate mothership, which is towing several small boats to be used in raids. Motherships enable pirates to stay at sea longer and attack merchant ships farther from shore.

captain's safe, crew members, or passengers; and then leave.

Somali pirates have been known to seize fishing vessels and *dhows* to use for another purpose: as motherships, or floating bases from which they can travel far from shore to conduct raids using their smaller boats. The larger vessels can carry extra pirates and weapons, along with several weeks' worth of food and fuel. Attack skiffs are often tied to the motherships.

By using motherships, pirates can stay out at sea for long periods of time and attack vessels as far as 1,000 miles offshore. As the use of motherships has become more common, the pirate danger area in the Indian Ocean has expanded.

When pirates seize large commercial vessels, they may try to unload valuable cargo and sell it on land. Sometimes, they will want not only the cargo, but also the ship itself to use for criminal purposes. In the Straits of Malacca, hijackers working for organized crime syndicates based in Asia, the United States, and Europe have targeted ships carrying such products as refined palm oil, kerosene, diesel fuel, rubber, steel, copper, and aluminum.

After selling the cargo, these pirates may try to turn the vessel into a "phantom ship." They will give the ship a new identity by painting over its name and other identifying features. International law requires that commercial vessels must display the flag of the country in which they are legally registered, or licensed. Ships must abide by the laws of their flag state. Pirates will circumvent this by forging false registry papers in the new name, often with a different flag state. These phantom ships are commonly used for smuggling, often of drugs or illegal immigrants.

In recent years, pirates have found that they can make the most money by holding a commercial vessel, along with its cargo and crew, for ransom. After taking control of a ship, pirates may bring the captured vessel back to a haven like Harardhere or Hobyo in Somalia. There, the hijacked vessels can be anchored offshore while the pirates negotiate through intermediaries with the ship's owner, families of the crewmembers, or both. In attempting to trade hostages for ransom, pirates have shown themselves willing to wait months for a satisfactory agreement. Hostages are often held in unpleasant conditions and fed poorly. Some have been handcuffed and beaten. A few hostages have died while in captivity.

The amounts of ransoms paid to Somali pirates have risen over the years. According to a study by the One Earth

An American sailor throws a bag containing illegal drugs over the side of a pirate skiff that the U.S. Navy intercepted during an antipiracy patrol in the Indian Ocean.

Three Yemeni fishermen cling to a piece of wood just before they are rescued in the Gulf of Aden by a U.S. patrol boat, November 2009. According to the fishermen, they were left stranded in the water after a dozen pirates hijacked their vessel. The fishermen said that the pirates gave them an ultimatum—jump overboard or be killed.

Future Foundation, in 2005 the average ransom payment was $150,000; by 2010 it was $5.4 million. Some hijacked oil tankers have been ransomed for $9 million or more.

Ransom payments are typically delivered by air, as shrink-wrapped packages of cash dropped from an airplane by parachute onto the deck of the hijacked vessel. After receiving payment Somali pirates generally abide by their agreements, releasing the captured ship and their hostages.

ECONOMIC COST OF PIRACY

In 2011 Somali pirates received a total of $160 million in ransom money. But that figure only represents a small portion of the total cost of piracy in that year. According to the One Earth Future Foundation, piracy along the Somali coast alone cost nearly $7 billion in 2011.

A large percentage of that money was spent by the shipping industry in antipiracy measures. For example, rerouting ships to avoid high-risk areas, and increasing speeds through dangerous areas cost shipping companies nearly $3.3 billion in 2011 due to higher fuel expenses. Another antipiracy effort is the installation of security equipment and hiring of privately hired armed guards, which was estimated to cost shipping companies $1.1 billion in 2011. Finally, the shipping companies had to pay higher insurance premiums when their ships traveled through waters designated as high risk. The two major kinds of insurance are war risk and kidnap and ransom. Their combined cost in 2011 was $635 million. Because of Somali piracy in January 2011 "war risk" regions included the Gulf of Aden, the Red Sea, the Gulf of Oman, and the Indian Ocean.

The shipping companies are not the only ones to pay a high price for piracy. Many state governments have spent millions of dollars each year to provide military protection to ships owned or operated by their citizens. In 2012 more than two dozen countries patrolled the coast of Somalia. The cost for international naval and aircraft antipiracy patrols was an estimated $1.2 billion.

Some analysts say the $7 billion annual price tag for battling Somali pirates falls short because it doesn't take into account the impact of piracy on the world's global health. About 80 percent of global commerce takes place by sea. If piracy closes down valuable shipping lanes, the economic cost to the world's economy could be several billions of dollars.

THE HUMAN COST OF PIRACY

Between 1998 and 2008 approximately 3,200 people were taken hostage at sea, with 500 of them wounded and 160 killed. Thousands more civilians and crew members became hostages during the more than 1,500 pirate attacks that took place after 2008.

According to an Oceans Beyond Piracy study, the hostages of Somali pirates spend on average more than eight months in captivity. Some of them are never released. They die from malnutrition, disease, or—driven mad by the ordeal of long captivity—suicide. Because hostages represent ransom money, Somali pirates traditionally treated crew members well. However, around the mid-2010s some Somali pirate gangs began to treat hostages brutally. They locked crew members in the ship's freezer, subjected them to mock executions, or actually killed them. In some cases pirates continued to hold crew members on land even after ransoms were paid.

In 2010 53 ships were hijacked around the world, with 49 of them captured off the coast of Somalia. One Earth Future reported that year there was a record 1,181 people held hostage. The following year 1,118 hostages languished in captivity and 24 died.

In 2012, the IMB reported there had been more than 270 pirate attacks worldwide, with 27 of them resulting in hijackings. Thirteen of those hijacking were by Somali pirates, who took 212 hostages.

2

ALONDRA RAINBOW
THE PHANTOM SHIP

One example of a raid in which pirates intended to create a "phantom ship" that they could use for smuggling was the hijacking of the MV *Alondra Rainbow* in Southeast Asia. On October 22, 1999, this Japanese-owned cargo ship, registered in Panama, left the port of Kuala Tanjung, Indonesia, carrying 7,000 metric tons of aluminum ingots. The vessel and its cargo, which were bound for Miike, Japan, were valued at around $20 million.

Soon after departing, the ship encountered pirates. In the Straits of Malacca, off the coast of the Indonesian island of Sumatra, 15 masked men armed with pistols, long-bladed knives (called *parang* knives), and swords forced their way onto the freighter. The pirates took over the *Alondra Rainbow* and set its crew of two Japanese officers and 15 Filipino seamen adrift in a lifeboat, along with basic provisions. About 10 days later Thai fishermen found the men and took them to safety in Phuket, Thailand.

By October 29 the *Alondra Rainbow* had become a phantom ship. The pirates re-painted the entire vessel, changing its name to MV *Mega Rama*. They had fake papers that indicated the ship was registered in Belize. The events marked a growing trend in which pirates were targeting ships, and not simply robbing crew members of their valuables. The incident was seen as a serious threat to the shipping business.

The hijacking of the *Alondra Rainbow* had been reported to the International Maritime Bureau (IMB), and word went out that the ship's owner had issued a reward for the safe return of the vessel, crew, and cargo. IMB's Piracy Reporting Center (PRC), based in Kuala Lumpur, Malaysia, proved vital assistance in finding and tracking the missing ship. IMB director Pottengal Mukundan told the *New York Times*, "The Kuala Lumpur center sent out a piracy alert to ships at sea, and they were able to track the hijacked vessel as ship after ship reported back that they had spotted the suspect vessel."

On November 14 an Indian Coast Guard plane spotted a ship fitting the description of the missing *Alondra Rainbow*. It was about 270 miles off India's southernwestern coast, near Goa. When they contacted the ship, the coast guard officers were told that it was the *Mega Rama*, and that the vessel would not stop because it was behind schedule. The pirates on board the ship said that they were traveling to a port in the United Arab Emirates. However, the Indian coast guard checked out the information and quickly determined that it was false.

Over the next three days both the coast guard patrol ship *Tarabai* and the

An Indian Coast Guard vessel fires on the MV *Alondra Rainbow*, disguised as the *Mega Rama*.

missile-armed Indian Navy warship *Prahar* gave chase. Both ships opened fire on the hijacked vessel, but were unable to intercept the freighter.

After the *Prahar* strafed the rear section of the ship with gunfire, the Indonesian pirates finally stopped the freighter. They then attempted to scuttle the vessel by setting it on fire and flooding its engine room. At that point Coast Guard troops stormed aboard and arrested the pirates.

The ship had been so badly damaged that it required repairs before it could be moved. It was towed to Mumbai, India, where it was determined that about half of its original cargo remained. It was believed that the rest had been sold in Cambodia or Thailand.

The captured pirate crew was brought to trial in India. The men received sentences of seven years in prison for the hijacking.

Indian sailors who rescued the *Alondra Rainbow* from pirates in 1999.

3

An American Sea Hawk helicopter flies over a suspected pirate vessel towing a skiff during an antipiracy patrol near the Gulf of Aden.

ANTIPIRACY EFFORTS

Concerns for the safety of sailors and for the health of the global economy, which depends heavily on maritime trade, has motivated governments and the shipping industry to develop new methods to prevent modern piracy. Nations have combined their naval forces, forming antipiracy task forces, while commercial shipping companies have developed practices that prevent ship boardings and—when a ship is seized—help crews survive. Such efforts include giving special training to crew members, making expensive modifications to ships, and hiring armed guards. A number of antipiracy organizations are also helping ships and their crews by providing information on dangerous regions to avoid and by coordinating antipiracy efforts.

INTERNATIONAL NAVAL PATROLS IN SOUTHEAST ASIA

By June 2005 the problem of piracy in the Straits of Malacca had become so serious that the region was designated a global danger zone by the Joint War Committee, an organization that works with major ship insurance companies such as Lloyds of London. The "high-risk" declaration meant that insurance companies would charge much higher premiums for any ships traveling through that area. Expensive insurance premiums would make shipping more expensive, and therefore less appealing to consumers, which threatened the trade-based economies of countries adjacent to the Straits of Malacca: Indonesia, Malaysia, and Singapore.

Those three nations had already begun to crack down on the piracy problem in 2004, when they joined together to create the Malacca Straits Patrols (MSP). This is a regional operation intended to keep the Straits of Malacca free from pirates. Thailand joined the MSP in 2008.

Countries that participate in the MSP conduct coordinated naval and air patrols of the straits. Each nation polices its own territorial waters, but all information about pirate activity is shared. The effort proved so successful in reducing piracy in the region that the war-risk designation was dropped in August 2006. In 2011, the number of pirate attacks in the Straits of Malacca reported to the International Maritime Bureau (IMB) was zero.

INTERNATIONAL NAVAL PATROLS IN THE GULF OF ADEN

Because Somalia has not had a strong central government since 1991, and does not have a naval force that could discourage attacks and hijackings in its territorial waters (defined as 12 nautical miles from the coast), piracy has thrived around the Horn of Africa. In the mid-2000s, Somali pirates often went unchallenged when operating within territorial waters. In effect, the pirates were safe from arrest because under international law, foreign naval vessels need the permission of a government to enter its territorial waters.

As Somali pirates began venturing into international waters, the governments of countries whose ships and citizens were being attacked took action. They established three major multinational operations to fight pirates from east Africa. The three forces work together, along with independently deployed naval warships from countries like China, France, India, Malaysia, and Russia that also patrol shipping lanes in international waters around the Gulf of Aden and the Indian Ocean. It is a challenging task, as the warships are responsible for protecting an area of more than 2 million square miles of sea.

One of the foremost of these groups is Combined Task Force 151, which is part of a larger international naval partnership, led by the United States, called Combined Maritime Forces (CMF). The United States, France, Germany, Japan, Spain, Turkey, and the United Kingdom, along with 18 other CMF member nations, all provide naval warships and aircraft that patrol shipping lanes to prevent acts of terrorism and piracy.

Combined Maritime Forces, which is based in Bahrain, was formed in February 2002 as a partnership of allied nations with the goal of fighting terrorism. It soon set up Combined Task Force 150 (CTF-150), which was ordered to patrol the Arabian Sea and the east coast of Africa. In January 2009 the focus of CTF-150 was redefined as counter-terrorism and maritime security, and a new task force, Combined Task Force 151, was established to focus specifically on preventing and disrupting attacks by Somali pirates.

The number of vessels, aircraft, and personnel assigned to CTF-151 varies depending on perceived need and their assignment from various countries. Command of CTF-151 is rotated among participatory nations.

A second antipiracy force is Operation Ocean Shield, which was established by the North Atlantic Treaty Organization (NATO), a military alliance of North American and European countries. This task force deploys warships to protect ships passing through the Gulf of Aden. Launched in August 2009, the antipiracy effort replaced Operation Allied Protector, a NATO operation begun in October 2008 in which warships escorted ships carrying supplies for the United Nations' World Food Programme (WFP), which was providing resources to help alleviate the humanitarian crisis in Somalia. Although not members of

An American warship follows a *dhow* suspected of being a pirate vessel in the Indian Ocean.

American patrol boats that are part of Combined Task Force 151 approach Yemeni *dhows* suspected of pirate activity in the Red Sea.

NATO, China and South Korea have sent warships to assist with Operation Ocean Shield.

The third antipiracy force is Operation Atalanta, which was established by the European Union's Naval Force Somalia (EU NAVFOR). The European Union created this joint naval task force in December 2008 to fight Somali piracy in the waters off the Horn of Africa. The original goal of Operation Atalanta was to escort World Food Programme vessels and protect commercial shipping from pirate attacks. In March 2012 EU NAVFOR expanded its mandate to also targeting pirate bases and equipment along the Somali coast. The EU forces have been willing to follow pirates up to 1.2 miles (2 km) inland in Somalia.

In addition to actively hunting pirates, and to responding when ships report they are under attacks, the warships of the three antipiracy task forces also provide protection for merchant vessels as they travel through the Gulf of Aden and the Indian Ocean. Ships are told to remain in a designated stretch of water known as the International Recommended Transit Corridor (IRTC), and this channel is patrolled regularly by warships and aircraft. Vessels that remain in this narrow sea lane can expect a quick response from a naval patrol if pirates should appear.

Representatives of the international antipiracy task forces operating in east Africa meet four times a year. At these meetings they discuss tactics and share information about pirates.

PREVENTING PIRATES FROM BOARDING

One way to keep pirates off a ship is to avoid regions where hijacking incidents have been reported. Some shipping companies have simply rerouted their ships to avoid pirate-infested waters. But this method can be very expensive because it takes more time and fuel for ships to travel around these areas.

When a vessel must enter dangerous waters, there are several protective measures the captain can take. Ideally, the ship could travel with other vessels in a convoy. Whether in a convoy or alone, the crew should maintain 24-hour pirate watches. If a ship is approached, the captain can try to escape pirate skiffs by increasing his vessel's speed and using evasive maneu-

Members of a visit, board, search and seizure (VBSS) team search for pirates inside a ship during a training exercise.

The British warship HMS *Cumberland* passes across the bow of a pirate mothership in an attempt to stop the vessel in the Gulf of Aden, November 2008. The pirates had been interrupted in their attack on a Danish merchant ship. They were arrested and their vessel seized. The *Cumberland* was operating as part of NATO's Operation Ocean Shield.

vers. Zigzagging a large ship back and forth can create a large wake that can swamp a small pirate vessel. Crew members should also be trained in ways to prevent pirates from boarding, such as blasting pre-charged fire hoses or water cannons at bandits attempting to climb up the ship's side.

More and more shipping companies are installing permanent barriers to illegal boarding. Antipiracy measures include removing ladders from the ship's lowest point of access (usually the stern), and installing netting, razor wire, and electrified fencing in these areas. Other ship modifications that can prevent pirates from taking control of a vessel is installing stronger bridge and engine room doors that cannot be opened from the outside.

Using Armed Guards

Many private maritime security companies offer protection forces and security personnel. But the use of armed guards on ships is controversial. Insurance companies endorse the practice. They reduce the insurance premiums paid by shipping companies that use private armed security on their ships.

Not everyone believes that merchant ships should carry armed guards. Critics of the practice say that the presence of guards can lead to greater violence and increase the risk that crew members will be injured or killed in battles with pirates. Also, there have been a few cases in which innocent fishermen have been mistaken for pirates, fired on, and killed.

Vessels must abide by the laws of the nation in which they are registered, and some flag states do not allow private armed guards. Ships must also abide by the laws in the countries where they dock. Maritime security providers have been arrested and jailed in Somalia, Egypt, and Kenya for bringing guns into the country.

Nevertheless the year 2011 saw a sharp increase in the use of private security forces, as several countries, including the United States and the United Kingdom, changed policies to support the use of armed security on ships. Other flag states that permit private armed security guards include Denmark, Germany, India, Italy, and Spain. By October 2012, about 80 percent of container ships and tankers sailing in the Indian Ocean were carrying armed guards. To date, no commercial ship with security guards has been successfully hijacked.

Installing a Safe Room

A ship modification that can save lives is the "safe room," sometimes referred to as the citadel. This is a secure area in which crew members can barricade themselves against pirates who have successfully boarded and are trying to take them hostage. Safe rooms are usually stocked with food and drinks, medical equipment, and other supplies. Contact with the outside world is possible via satellite phone.

On September 9, 2010, a safe room on the cargo ship *Magellan Star* kept its crew from being taken hostage during an attack by Somali pirates off the coast of Yemen. The container ship was en route from Spain to Vietnam, when nine pirates seized the ship, despite the fact that it was traveling as part of a convoy escorted by warships. Two American warships and a Turkish frigate quickly surrounded the vessel, while U.S. Navy helicopters hovered overhead. The ship was dead in the water, as the captain had stopped the engine and disabled the controls so the pirates could not sail the *Magellan Star* away. However, the pirates refused to surrender.

In most cases, naval patrols would not try to free a hijacked vessel by force because of the risk that crew members held hostage could be injured or killed by the pirates. The military would instead allow ship owners to negotiate a ransom with the pirates. But because the 11 sailors of the *Magellan Star* were hidden in the ship's safe room, soldiers from the American warships USS *Dubuque* and USS *Princeton* took action. Two dozen U.S. Marine commandos stormed the ship. They arrested the pirates without firing a single shot.

INSTALLING SATELLITE TRACKING

If a ship has been hijacked, another useful piece of security equipment is a satellite-tracking device. Such systems can be used to follow a hijacked ship, especially one that has been turned into a phantom ship. One ship security alert system, the ShipLoc, enables ship owners to monitor the location of their vessel via the Internet anywhere in the world.

ANTIPIRACY ORGANIZATIONS

Several organizations work to ensure the safety of seafarers. Some of these groups monitor the passage of ships through high-risk areas. Others record reports of pirate attacks and hijackings, while also disseminating information about combating piracy.

The International Maritime Bureau (IMB) was established in 1981 by the International Chamber of Commerce. This London-based organization focuses on crime related to shipping and trade. It compiles statistics on maritime crime and publishes a weekly piracy report, as well as quarterly and annual reports on piracy and armed robbery at sea.

In 1992 the IMB established the Piracy Reporting Center (PRC), which is based in Kuala Lumpur, Malaysia. The PRC is a free 24-hour service that allows seafarers to report attacks, robberies, or suspicious behavior observed at sea. As a continuously manned monitoring service, the center constantly receives and disseminates reports of piracy and armed robbery occurring around the world. Its purpose is to inform people involved with the shipping industry about areas at high risk for pirate attacks and specific seaports associated with armed robberies on ships. The PRC also works closely with government officials and law enforcement authorities in allocating resources necessary to stop piracy and armed robbery on the seas. Reporting by both the IMB and the PRC is said to have foiled piracy attempts and led to the recovery of many hijacked vessels.

The International Maritime Organization (IMO), based in London, is an agency of the United Nations. The IMO works to provide information and enact regulations related to marine safety. Such subjects include ship passenger safety, ship pollution, the training and certification of ship crews, and ship security. The organization has also provided guidelines on piracy, including suggestions on how to protect ships from pirate attacks.

Traditionally, the International Maritime Organization has discouraged merchant ships from carrying armed guards, or from providing firearms to sailors for protection. However, in May 2012 agency officials acknowledged that the growing threat of piracy meant that new IMO guidelines with regard to armed guards were urgently needed. "International standards or regimes should be established," IMO secretary general Koji Sekimizu explained. "That regime should not be made compulsory, but provide an international framework on which the flag state and the [shipping] companies may decide to employ arms on board."

The Maritime Security Center–Horn of Africa (MSCHOA) was an initiative established by the European Union naval force in Somalia. It provides 24-hour manned monitoring of vessels traveling through the Gulf of Aden, off the Horn of Africa, or in the Somali Basin. Up-to-date information about incidents in the region are provided on the MSCHOA website, which also allows commercial ships to register their locations with the center.

In November 2004, 16 countries signed the Regional Cooperation Agreement on Combating Piracy and

Helicopters that can land and take off from the deck of a ship allow antipiracy task forces to cover larger areas of the ocean than the warships would normally be capable of patrolling.

Armed Robbery against ships in Asia (ReCAAP). This was a effort to coordinate antipiracy efforts and share information. The agreement established an Information Sharing Center, which publishes a monthly report and maintains a website on piracy-related information. Today, 17 countries are members of ReCAAP, including Bangladesh, Brunei, Cambodia, China, Denmark, India, Japan, South Korea, Laos, Myanmar, the Netherlands, Norway, the Philippines, Singapore, Sri Lanka, Thailand, the United Kingdom, and Vietnam.

CHOIZIL HIJACKING
TWENTY MONTHS IN "HOSTAGE HELL"

A South African couple working as crew on a small yacht saw their journey from Dar-es-Salaam, Tanzania, back home to South Africa turn into a nightmare when they fell into the hands of Somali pirates. Bruno Pelizzari and Debbie Calitz would endure one of the longest periods of captivity experienced by hostages of Somali pirates.

Peter Eldridge was captain of the *Choizil*, a yacht that he had built and lived on for several years in Dar-es-Salaam. In the fall of 2010, knowing that Pelizzari and Calitz had family in South Africa, he invited them to serve as crew on his yacht for a trip to Richards Bay, South Africa.

The yacht and its three seafarers were sailing off the coast of Tanzania on October 26, 2010, when the *Choizil* was attacked. Two speedboats pulled up on each side of the yacht. Eldridge

quickly sent out a Mayday signal, but that didn't stop 12 pirates, armed with AK-47 rifles and RPGs, from boarding the yacht. They took the ship's radio, as well as money and valuables from the three crew members. Eldridge expected that after robbing them, the pirates would leave. But they stayed on the yacht. A pirate mothership brought food and other supplies to the pirates as they sailed north toward Somalia.

Eldridge, Pelizzari, and Calitz had been held hostage for nearly two weeks when the yacht was approached by warships—one from France and the other from the Netherlands. The pirates fired rockets at the French ship. Then they held guns to the heads of their hostages and told Eldridge to inform the French warship by radio that pirates had taken control of the yacht.

The ships followed as the *Choizil* sailed to the Somali coast, where it ran aground. Dutch military helicopters circled as the pirates ordered their three hostages to get off the boat. Eldridge, who would later say he was prepared to die on his yacht, refused. But Pelizzari and Calitz were forced off and dragged away. They heard a Somali pirate arguing with the stubborn captain, who was clinging to a bulkhead. After hearing a gun fired, they would later explain, they thought Eldridge had been killed.

But the bullet missed and the pirate fled. Eldridge was rescued by the Dutch navy, which also arrested five of the Somali pirates. The captain, his yacht, and the five Somalis were first taken to Richard's Bay. When South African officials refused to prosecute the pirates, the five Somalis were transported to the Netherlands and tried for piracy in a Dutch court. In August 2011 the five pirates were sentenced to prison for terms of up to seven years.

Meanwhile, Bruno Pelizzari and Debbie Calitz remained in the pirates' hands. The pirates did not treat the hostages well. They were given little food, handcuffed most of the time, forced to remain in darkness, moved from house to house, and regularly beaten. Calitz would later write a book about her experience, describing it as "hostage hell."

The pirates who had captured Pelizzari and Calitz demanded a huge ransom of $10 million. Neither the cou-

Bruno Pelizzari and Debbie Calitz celebrate their release after being held for nearly 20 months.

ple nor their families had access to that much money, although relatives in South Africa tried to raise money for the ransom by holding fundraisers and asking for donations. Months went by as the pirates negotiated with family members and government officials from the Transitional Federal Government of Somalia, South Africa, and Italy. (Pelizzari was a citizen of Italy as well as South Africa.)

It would not be until June 2012 that Pelizzari and Calitz were finally released. Somali government officials said that the couple had been freed through the intervention of Somalia's military. Other sources reported that their release came about after a ransom had been paid.

5

Cruise ships make challenging targets because of their large size. That has not stopped some audacious pirates from attempting attacks, however.

CRUISE SHIP ATTACKS

Pirates seldom attack cruise ships. The massive size of these vessels makes them difficult to board and they typically contain hundreds of crew members and passengers, who would be difficult for pirates to subdue and control. Cruise ship companies have established security standards to prevent attacks, as well as procedures for sailors to follow in the event of an attempted boarding.

One pirate attack on a cruise ship occurred in November 2005. The Bahamas-registered *Seabourn Spirit* had left Alexandria, Egypt, bound for Mombasa, Kenya. It carried around 300 passengers and crew members. At around 5:30 A.M. on November 5, 2005, passengers on the vessel were awakened by the sound of gunfire.

Some people would later place blame for the attack on the captain for bringing the cruise ship too close to the African coast. At the time maritime security groups recommended that ships maintain a distance of 200 miles off the east coast of Africa to avoid pirates. The *Seabourn Spirit* was traveling about 100 miles off the coast when it was attacked.

But the captain was also credited for his work in preventing the pirates from boarding. As two 25-foot rigid inflatable boats loaded with men waving rocket-propelled grenades and machine guns threatened the ship, the captain immediately began evasive maneuvers. He ordered the ship to be steered back and forth. This would create a wake that he hoped would swamp the attacking boats. For their safety, passengers were ordered to stay in the main ballroom. They would later describe hearing bullets striking the ship's hull.

In addition to shooting at the ship with their AK-47 rifles, at one point the

The motor from a rocket-propelled grenade embedded itself in a bulkhead on the *Seabourn Spirit* while the cruise liner was being attacked by pirates off the coast of Somalia in November 2005.

pirates fired a pair of rocket-propelled grenades at the *Seabourn Spirit*. One struck a bulkhead and exploded. Flying debris injured a crew member. The other bounced off the ship's stern, causing no damage.

The pirates broke off their violent attack after crew members set up and turned on a special long-range acoustic device (LRAD). This sonic weapon emits extremely intense, ear-splitting sounds that focused on the pirate boats, quickly forcing them to withdraw. The ship increased its speed and left them behind.

Three years would pass before Somali pirates tried another cruise liner attack. In December 2008 two small

fishing boats attempted to intercept the cruise liner *Nautica*, which was on a 32-day voyage from Rome to Singapore. The liner, which carried 690 passengers and a crew of 386, was in the Gulf of Aden when pirate boats tried to close in on it. Attackers in one boat fired shots from rifles from a distance of about 300 yards. The captain of the *Nautica* responded by taking evasive action, and the cruise ship soon outran the boats. No one was injured in the attack.

In April 2009 armed security guards fired back when pirates attacked the Italian cruise ship *MSC Melody*. The cruise ship was carrying around 1,000 passengers and 500 crew members on a 22-day cruise from Durban, South Africa, to Genoa, Italy. The *Melody* was about 200 miles north of the Seychelles, and about 500 miles east of Somalia, when it was threatened by a small boat carrying six men firing automatic weapons.

The *MSC Melody* was protected by armed guards, who exchanged gunfire with the attackers. Passengers also threw deck chairs at the pirates when they tried to climb up the side of the ship. The hijacking was prevented, and the vessel continued on its way without any reported injuries and only minor damage to the ship.

In January 2011 the British cruise ship *Spirit of Adventure* encountered trouble while carrying 350 passengers and a crew of 200 from Madagascar to Zanzibar, Tanzania. The cruise ship was about 100 miles off the coast of Zanzibar when it was met by a speedboat carrying armed men. As the small boat pulled alongside the cruise ship, the captain ordered the passengers, who had just sat down to dinner, to take

shelter in a lounge below the deck. The ship then took evasive maneuvers while crew members fired a water cannon at the pirate speedboat.

Ultimately, the pirates did not fire at the ship, and although they traveled very close for about 10 minutes, they did not attempt to board. The passengers were able to resume their dinner about an hour later. Later the passengers would learn that, on the same day, pirates had captured a cargo ship about 15 miles away from the *Spirit of Adventure* and sailed it away, demanding a ransom.

Armed security guards enabled the Italian cruise ship *MSC Melody* to escape an attack by six pirates armed with AK-47 rifles in April 2009.

6

With modern pirates continuing to target supertankers, it has become more likely that large amounts of oil could be vented into the sea, causing an environmental disaster.

ENVIRONMENTAL THREAT OF PIRACY

The possibility of a massive oil spill resulting from piracy has grown as pirates gain access to more and more powerful weapons. Whenever pirates board an oil tanker, there is a threat of serious environmental damage due to the ship running aground or colliding with another vessel.

Such a situation came close to happening in early 1999 when the *Chaumont*, a French-flagged oil tanker (designated a "very large crude carrier," or VLCC) was hijacked. The *Chaumont* was traveling from the Persian Gulf to the Philippines with a cargo of crude oil when pirates attacked the ship in Phillip Channel, an area of the Straits of Malacca near Singapore. While the pirates subdued and tied up the crew, the *Chaumont* continued to motor along with no one at the helm, traveling at top speed through one of the world's busiest shipping lanes. According to various reports, the *Chaumont* remained without out anyone at the helm for between 35 and 70 minutes. If the ship had run aground or collided with another vessel, it could have caused massive oil damage to the region.

As pirates have become more daring, targeting VLCCs in order to collect large ransoms, the potential for devastating oil spills increases. In an October 2008 report, the London-based organization Chatham House warned of possible dangers: "A tanker could be set on fire, sunk, or forced ashore, any of which could result in an environmental catastrophe that would devastate marine and bird life for years to come."

A month after the Chatham House report was published, Somali pirates seized their first oil tanker, the *Sirius Star*. This VLCC, owned by a subsidiary of Saudi Aramco (the Saudi Arabian oil company), was the largest ship ever captured by pirates to that point. The *Sirius Star* was held for about two months until a $3 million ransom was paid by the owners. (For more on the *Sirius Star* hijacking, see page 71.)

The ransom amount would rise dramatically with the next supertanker hijacking, that of the *Maran Centaurus* in November 2009. The ship was traveling from Kuwait to oil refineries at Louisiana in the United States with a load of crude oil valued at more than $150 million. It was 570 nautical miles northeast of the Seychelles when it was captured. The pirates directed the ship to the coast of Somalia, where it was anchored at Harardhere, near the port of Hobyo, an infamous haven for pirates. The *Maran Centaurus* was held there for 47 days, until it was ransomed.

The actual amount of the ransom paid is unknown, though it was high. The pirates apparently received between $5 and $7 million in cash from the vessel's owners, which was air-dropped onto the ship. However, some reports indicated that the pirates may also have received another $2 million via bank wire transfer.

Very large crude carriers (VLCCs) such as this one can carry around 250,000 deadweight tons of petroleum—the equivalent of more than 2 million barrels of oil. With the price of oil at $75 to $90 per barrel, the value of a supertanker's cargo can exceed $150 million, making the enormous ships a tempting target for pirates.

A few months later, in April 2010, Somali pirates hijacked a South Korean VLCC that was carrying oil from Iraq to the United States. The pirates captured the *Samho Dream* and sailed it to Harardhere, where the supertanker was anchored for more than 200 days. In November 2010 the pirates received a ransom believed to be $9 million, and turned the ship back over to its owners.

Somali pirates captured their fourth VLCC in February 2011 when they hijacked the *Irene SL*. This Greek-owned oil tanker was seized about 220 miles off Oman. The supertanker and its 25 crew members had left Kuwait, bound for the United States with a cargo of 2 million barrels of crude oil—worth around $200 million. It was one of the richest cargos ever taken by pirates, and was ransomed 58 days later for a record $13.5 million.

Another VLCC hijacking by Somali pirates took place in May 2012. The Greek-owned Liberian-flagged *Smyrni*, which was carrying 135,000 tons of oil valued at $115 million, was seized while cruising off the coast of Oman. Reports indicated that two skiffs carrying 10 pirates armed with automatic weapons had been prevented from boarding the tanker at first. But on their second attempt, the determined pirates managed to board. The oil tanker, with its 26-man crew aboard, was taken to Somalia, where it was held for ransom through the end of 2012.

After pirates released the supertanker *Irene SL*, crew members worked with the international police force Interpol in an effort to identify the hijackers. They were able to identify four of the pirates, who were subsequently arrested and prosecuted for piracy by the Greek government in late 2012 and early 2013.

7

FAINA HIJACKING
DANGEROUS CARGO

In 2008 Somali pirates seized 42 ships. Their 26th hijacking that year, in which they captured the Belize-flagged Ukrainian cargo ship *Faina*, brought the pirates to the attention of the world. When the *Faina* was hijacked on September 25 about 200 miles off the coast of Somalia, the 50 or so men who took over the vessel discovered that it held more than $30 million worth of weapons. The cargo included 33 Russian T-72 battle tanks, 150 rocket launchers, and 6 antiaircraft guns.

Concerns over what would happen to the dangerous cargo made national headlines. In 2008 the U.S.-supported Somali Transitional Federal Government (TFG) was fighting against an Islamist insurgency. U.S. and Somali government officials worried that the weapons would fall into the hands of the insurgents. The U.S. Navy was directed to find the *Faina* quickly, and within three days the warship USS *Howard* closed in on the vessel. The hijacked ship had been moored off the coastal town of Harardhere, a pirate haven that already held several other hijacked vessels. Warships from the U.S. Fifth Fleet would continue to surround the hijacked vessel during the time it was held by the pirates. They allowed food and water to be taken onboard but their presence was to prevent the removal of any cargo.

The Somali pirates insisted that the hijacking of the *Faina* was just business. The Ukrainian ship had not been targeted because of its military cargo, but was taken only by chance, a spokesman for the pirate group, Sugule Ali, told a reporter for the *New York Times*. The pirate skiff had simply been waiting in the busy Gulf of Aden when a large blue and white ship with ropes hanging off its side slowly passed by. Sugule insisted that the pirates wanted only money.

In September 2008 Somali pirates in small boats were able to hijack the MV *Faina*, a cargo ship carrying a load of T-72 tanks and other weapons.

That ransom payment, he said, would be used to help clean up the hazardous waste, including nuclear waste, that foreign companies were illegally dumping off the Somali coast. He explained:

> We don't consider ourselves sea bandits ["sea bandit" is one way Somalis translate the English word *pirate*]. We consider sea bandits those who illegally fish in our seas and dump waste in our seas and carry weapons in our seas. We are simply patrolling our seas. Think of us like a coast guard.

In addition to the *Faina*, the Central Region Coast Guard (as the pirate group called itself) was holding 20 crew members hostage—17 Ukrainian nationals, two Russians, and one Latvian. A 21st crew member, the Russian captain, had died a few days after the hijacking, reportedly of hypertension. In the press, reports of the pirates' initial ransom demand for the release of the ship and its crew ranged from $5 million to $35 million. Officials from the Ukraine, Somalia, Russia, the United States, and Britain worked together in trying to speed negotiations.

Pirates armed with rocket-propelled grenades (RPGs) on the deck of the *Faina*, October 2008.

As ransom talks dragged on, the *Faina* hostages began to fear for their lives. In November Ukrainian members of the crew sent an email to a journal in Kiev in which they voiced their desperation. After writing that they were running out of fuel, water and food, the captives said: "The last warning of the soldiers [pirates] is that if the ransom demands are not satisfied, the cargo and crew will be destroyed."

After four months of negotiations the ship owners and pirates reached an agreement. On February 4, 2009, a cash payment of $3.2 million was made, dropped by parachute into the water near the ship. It was the largest ransom amount ever paid at that time.

The following day the ship and crew were released, and they headed to Mombasa, under the escort of the U.S. Navy. The Kenyan government had issued a statement claiming that the cargo belonged to Kenya, having been purchased for its military forces.

(Top) Pirates guard the crew of *Faina* in November 2008, while the ship is anchored off the coast of Somalia.

(Bottom) Ransom money is dropped in the vicinity of *Faina* on February 4, 2009. The pirates left the merchant ship a day later, escaping with $3.2 million.

8

PIRACY IN THE GULF OF GUINEA

The countries of Benin, Cameroon, Equatorial Guinea, Gabon, Ghana, Nigeria, and Togo border the Gulf of Guinea, a maritime region that is important to the shipping industry. Valuable goods such as oil, gold, bauxite, iron ore, and farm products pass through the Gulf of Guinea on their way to Europe, the United States, and South America. Piracy has been a problem in this region for decades, but the problem has grown worse over the past few years.

During the early 1990s most pirate attacks in West African ports were limited to robbing seafarers of cash and jewelry. But by the end of that decade West African pirates began to grow bolder. Nigeria is one of the world's major oil producers, but much of its oil is shipped to foreign countries where it is refined into gasoline and other products. Daring West African pirates began to take control of supertankers while

they were near the coast and siphon off oil for sale on the black market. Crew members might be detained for a few hours, or sometimes several days, while the pirates transferred the cargo to their own tankers, or to containers in smaller vessels.

It was fairly rare for pirates to take hostages in the late 1990s and early 2000s. However, such incidents did occur. For example, in July 1999 the Bahamanian-flagged tanker *Kilchem Oceania* was seized off Lagos, Nigeria, by 20 armed pirates. After stealing valuable items from the ship, the pirates took two Russian crew members hostage. Intense negotiations, and payment of a ransom, led to the men's release a month later.

Since 2009 the Gulf of Guinea has seen a growing number of kidnappings for ransom. Overall, pirate attacks, whether for cargo or ransom payments, are on the rise in the Gulf of Guinea. According to one report, there were no pirate attacks in the waters off the coast of Benin in 2010, but 19 pirate attacks in 2011. A total of 64 ships reported being attacked by pirates in the Gulf of Guinea during 2011, compared to 45 pirate attacks the previous year. And these figures do not include many attacks that are not reported each year.

In August 2011 the London-based Joint War Committee, an organization composed of large companies that provide insurance for ships, designated the territorial waters of Benin as a "war-risk zone" because of the increased pirate danger there. The Joint War Committee also expanded a "pirate danger area" off the coast of Nigeria, which it had previously labeled as being very risky for

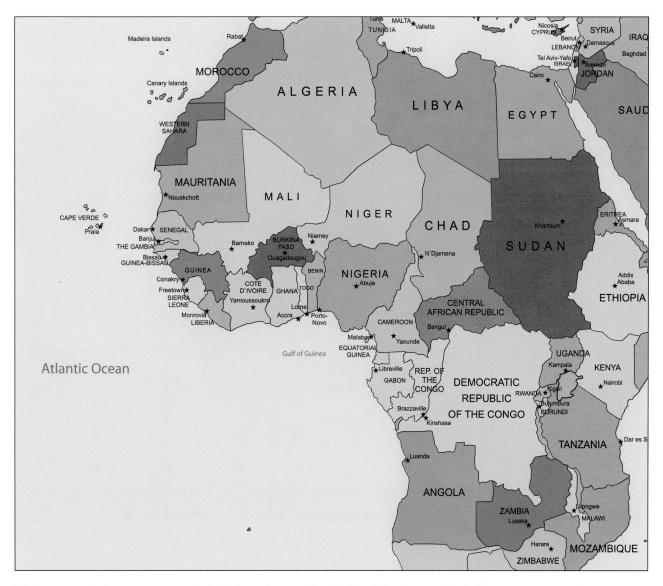

This map of the west coast of Africa shows the Gulf of Guinea, which in recent years has become known for increased pirate activity.

merchant vessels. In effect, these rulings meant that the waters off West Africa had become as dangerous to shipping as the waters around the Horn of Africa to the east.

The "high-risk" declaration significantly increases the amount of money shipping companies must pay to insure their vessels. This, in turn, has a serious impact on the economies of the major port cities of West Africa, including Cotonou and Porto Novo in Benin, and Lagos in Nigeria. According to one report, the revenue at Cotonou was down by 70 percent in 2012 due to revenue lost because of pirate activity. The war risk designation placed Nigeria, Benin, and nearby waters in the same risk category as Somalia.

But unlike Somalia, which has no effective central government, these West African countries have governments capable of enforcing laws against piracy in their waters. In response to the "high risk" insurance designation, in September 2011 Nigeria and Benin

A tanker passes an oil rig as it sails into the port at Lagos, Nigeria. The country is among the world's leading oil-producing nations, which has made Nigeria one of the wealthier countries in Africa. However, corruption has historically been widespread in Nigeria's government and among its law enforcement agencies, creating a situation in which pirates are able to raid shipping with little fear that they will be apprehended.

Naval officers from Cameroon, Congo, Ghana, and Nigeria discuss ways their navies can cooperate on antipiracy activities in the Gulf of Guinea, November 2012.

began working together on warship and helicopter patrols of the Gulf of Guinea. Their antipiracy mission was called Operation Prosperity. A commander with the Nigerian navy told the BBC, "Before Operation Prosperity, the Nigeria-Benin corridor was becoming extremely notorious. But the presence of the naval ships has reduced the crime significantly." The Nigerian government noted that there had been 35 pirate attacks in the territorial waters of Benin and Nigeria in the first nine months of 2011. From the start of Operation Prosperity until March 2012, there was only one reported pirate attack.

However, some analysts say that the patrols have not really reduced pirate activity, just moved it elsewhere in the Gulf. They note that around 2011 pirate groups became more organized, espe-

cially at targeting tankers using a mother ship from which to launch attacks in smaller boats outside of the territorial waters of Benin and Nigeria.

At the same time there have been more reports of violent pirate attacks in the Gulf of Guinea. In January 2012, for example, a Taiwanese-owned bulk cargo vessel, the *Fourseas SW*, was hit with a heavy spray of pirate gunfire, killing the captain and chief engineer. The following month eight heavily armed Nigerian pirates attacked the Dutch-owned cargo ship *Breiz Klipper* off the coast of Nigeria. The captain and chief engineer, both Russians, and a Filipino crew member were seized. All three hostages were released 25 days later, although news reports did not indicate whether a ransom was paid.

In October 2012 the French oil

The supertanker *Abu Dhabi Star*, which was hijacked by pirates in September 2012. Some experts believe the recent pirate hijackings of tanker ships in the Gulf of Guinea may be the work of a single criminal organization that has infiltrated Nigeria's oil and shipping industries.

transport vessel *Bourbon Liberty 249* was seized and seven of its crew members (six Russians and one Estonian) were taken off the vessel. They were held for two weeks before being ransomed. Apparently, the pirates had been interested only in kidnapping specific members of the crew—nine other sailors had been left on the vessel.

By September 2012, a year after Operation Prosperity had been started, more than 40 pirate attacks had been reported in the Gulf of Guinea. That month the cargo of the 600-foot-long tanker *Abu Dhabi Star* was stolen. This ship, which was carrying refined oil from Nigeria to the United States, was 12 nautical miles from Lagos when it

was attacked. By the time the 20 pirates boarded the ship in the darkness, the crew had fled to a safe room and sent out a distress signal. However, Nigerian naval forces did not respond for almost 12 hours. By the time a navy warship arrived, the pirates had vanished along with the ship's cargo.

In October 2012 a report by the International Maritime Bureau blamed Nigerian criminals for the rise in pirate hijackings in West Africa. Government officials in Benin have called on the United Nations to establish an international force to police the Gulf of Guinea waters, similar to the NATO and EU-led antipiracy efforts currently conducted off the coast of East Africa.

9

HOSTAGES SEIZED ON LAND

Although the kidnapping of people on land is technically not piracy, as this is defined by the UN Convention on the Law of the Sea, several kidnappings have occurred in Kenya and Somalia that are considered to be an offshoot of Somali piracy. Pirate gangs based in Somalia carried out the kidnappings and held their hostages captive in the country. In some cases Somali gunmen working for an Islamist insurgent group known as al-Shabaab (also spelled al-Shabab) have carried out kidnappings and later sold their hostages to Somali pirates based in Harardhere, a pirate haven on the coast of central Somalia.

JUDITH TEBBUTT: On September 11, 2011, just past midnight, British citizens David and Judith Tebbutt were awakened from their sleep by pirates who had entered their grass hut at a remote beach resort in northern Kenya. The two tourists had arrived the day before. They were the only guests at the exclusive Kiwayu Safari Village, located north of Lamu Island, not far from the Somali border. During a violent struggle 58-year-old David Tebbutt was shot dead while his 56-year-old wife Judith was dragged, screaming, down to the beach and onto a small speedboat. She would not learn until two weeks later that her husband had been killed.

Tebbutt had been kidnapped for ransom. She was taken by boat to the Kismayo region, in southern Somalia, and a few days later moved near the Somali coastal town of Harardhere. There, she would remain in captivity for six months. In March 2012 her son arranged her release by paying $1.2 million in ransom, which was air-dropped by plane. The five pirates who kidnapped Tebbutt were never found.

MARIE DEDIEU: On October 1 a 66-year-old disabled Frenchwoman named Marie Dedieu was kidnapped from her part-time home on the island of Manda near the Kenyan resort town of Lamu. Kenyan coast patrols pursued the kidnappers, who escaped with Dedieu into Somali waters. Dedieu was a diabetic with a serious heart condition. Denied access to needed medication she died in captivity on September 19 in southern Somalia. Pirates demanded a ransom for the release of her body.

MONTSERRAT SERRA AND BLANCA THIEBAUD: In October 2011 al-Shabaab Islamist militants kidnapped two Doctors Without Borders (MSF) aid workers from the Dadaab refugee camp in Northern Kenya. In January 2012 the two Spanish women—Montserrat Serra and Blanca Thiebaud—were sold for $200,000 to a pirate gang led by Mohamed Abdi Hassan, known simply as Afweyne. They were moved to Afweyne's pirate base of Harardhere, where they were still being held as of December 2012.

JESSICA BUCHANAN AND POUL THISTED: In October 2011, 32-year-old American Jessica Buchanan and 60-year

Members of a U.S. Navy visit, board, search and seizure (VBSS) team demonstrate how to approach a suspect vessel in the Gulf of Aden, 2012.

old Dane Poul Thisted were in Somalia working for the Danish Demining Group (DDG). After giving a talk in the town of Galkayo on ways to safely de-mine lands, the two left for the airport but while on the road they were kid-napped by a pirate gang. The hostages were held in various villages near Harardhere. For a time they were even imprisoned on a hijacked ship, the MV *Albedo*, which had been seized in November 2010. But they were later moved back to shore. The kidnappers wanted $10 million for their release.

Jessica Buchanan and Poul Hagen Thisted were held by Somali pirates for three months, before being rescued in an operation conducted by American special forces.

After U.S. government officials heard reports that Buchanan's health was deteriorating, plans were made to free the hostages. In January 2012 they were about 150 miles inland, in a remote area near the town of Gadaado, close to Ethiopia. At 3:30 in the morn-ing of January 25 Navy Seal special operations forces parachuted into the area and executed a tightly coordinated rescue operation. All nine kidnappers, who were heavily armed, were killed. The two hostages were rescued without harm and brought to safety.

Michael Scott Moore: A week before Buchanan and Thisted were res-cued by Navy Seals, journalist Michael Moore, who holds U.S. and German cit-izenship, had been kidnapped. Moore had written about piracy since 2008, but he had come to Somalia to write about World Food Programme work in the country. He had been in Somalia only two weeks when he was kidnapped on the same road that Buchanan and Thisted had been traveling when kid-napped three months earlier.

The aid workers' rescue angered the pirates holding Moore. His captors had initially demanded a ransom of $10 mil-lion for his release. They doubled their demand to $20 million. And they threatened to kill him if any rescue attempts were made. One of the pirate leaders, Hassan Abdi, told reporters: "If they try again, we will all die together." Reports indicate that Moore has been frequently moved from place to place, mostly in the area around Harardhere. As of December 2012 he remained a captive of Somali pirates.

Hostages Seized at Sea

For many years Somali pirates typically did not harm their captives. There was even a Somali pirate code of conduct requiring that captives not be abused. However, according to a 2012 study by Chatham House, pirate attacks off Somalia became increasingly violent beginning in the summer of 2010. Some pirate gangs began to carry out "example killings," to demonstrate that failure to comply could be deadly for crew members.

As ransom negotiations have dragged out, some people have been forced to spend years as prisoners, facing malnutrition, lack of medical attention, abuse, and violence. Among the hostage situations that have taken the longest to conclude are the *Iceberg I* hijacking, in March 2010; the *Albedo* hijacking, in November 2010; and the *Orna* hijacking, in December 2010.

The worst-case scenario for ransom negotiations is the hijacking of the Dubai-owned cargo ship *Iceberg I*. It has become the longest-held hijacked ship in modern maritime history.

The ship, bound for England, was reportedly carrying a cargo of generators, transformers, and empty fuel tanks when it was hijacked by Somali pirates on March 29, 2010, in the Gulf of Aden. At the time it was traveling outside the International Recommended Transit Corridor, and not in an area regularly patrolled by international naval forces. The 24 crew members aboard the vessel included nine Yemeni, six Indians, four Ghanaians, two Sudanese, two Pakistani, and one Filipino. Their ship, with them aboard as hostages, was anchored near the pirate stronghold of Hobyo.

The gang that captured the ship treated its crew brutally. One news report described horrific living conditions in which hostages were confined in a small room and given little food and clean water. After seven months of living in such dire conditions, the Yemeni third officer committed suicide by throwing himself overboard. In February 2011 another crewman disappeared when he was dragged off the ship by some of the pirates. Several hostages became ill and in December 2011 were moved off the ship to land. In periodic interviews with television stations or in rare phone calls with family, crew members pleaded for help and complained of being beaten and abused.

Throughout the crew's ordeal, the ship's Yemeni owner, Azal Shipping and Cargo, based in Dubai, refused to pay the ransom price. (The initial demand was $8 million.) In fact, the manage-

The American warship USS *Whidbey Island* (right) follows MV *Golden Nori*, a Panamanian-flagged chemical tanker captured by pirates in the fall of 2007. *Whidbey Island* had responded to the crew's distress call during the pirate attack, and arrived in time to sink two pirate skiffs. However, under the terms of a 1992 United Nations arms embargo, the warship was not permitted to follow *Golden Nori* into Somali territorial waters. The ship and 23-member crew were held for six weeks before their safe release. Six months after this incident, in June 2008, the UN Security Council unanimously passed a declaration authorizing nations that have the consent of Somalia's Transitional Federal Government to enter Somali territorial waters and deal with pirates.

ment of the company was accused of doing nothing to help the crew. Months passed before company officials met with hostage families. In July 2012 rumors that a $6 million ransom had been agreed on and paid led many relatives to become hopeful of their loved ones' safe return. However, as of mid-December 2012 the ship and crew were still being held hostage. Swedish filmmaker Neil Bell made a documentary released in 2011 of the hijacking and captivity of the *Iceberg I*.

Another ship to endure almost two years of captivity was the Malaysian tanker *Albedo*, which was hijacked in November 2010 while traveling in the Gulf of Aden. Its 23-member crew included men from Bangladesh, India, Iran, Pakistan, and Sri Lanka. The pirates demanded a ransom of $2.85 million but Pakistani families managed to raise only $1.2 million.

In August 2012, when that money was paid, seven Pakistani sailors were released. However, 15 other sailors remained prisoners of the pirates. One member of the crew had died of disease while in captivity.

Hijacked a month after the *Albedo*, in December 2010, the *Orna* was near the Seychelles when it was seized by Somali pirates. The Panama-flagged bulk cargo ship was anchored near the pirate haven of Harardhere while ransom negotiations for the release of the ships and hostages took place. The ship's 22-man crew lived on the ship until May 2011, when a fire in the kitchen forced them off.

The months passed and ransom discussions went poorly. In August 2012 one of the sailors was killed. Pirate leader Hassan Abdi claimed the man had been executed and another crewmember wounded to send a message to the owners of the ship to stop delaying the ransom payment. This is thought to be the first time pirates in Somalia killed a hostage because of failed ransom discussions.

The *Orna* and most of its crew were released in October 2012 after a $600,000 ransom was paid. However, six hostages were kept back by the pirates, who continue to hold the ship's captain, engineer, and four others on land.

LE PONANT HIJACKING
FRANCE RESPONDS TO PIRACY

On April 4, 2008, while en route from the Seychelles to Yemen, where it was to pick up passengers, the 288-foot-long, three-masted luxury yacht *Le Ponant* was captured by a dozen Somali pirates. The 32-cabin French yacht, which featured four decks and two restaurants, was capable of holding 64 passengers. However, at the time of its capture it carried just 30 crew members, 22 of whom were French.

The pirates took the crew hostage and demanded a hefty ransom of $2 million from the ship's owners, the French charter company CMA-CGM. They moored the yacht near the port of Eyl, a pirate haven located in the semi-autonomous Puntland region of northeastern Somalia. Negotiations were quickly concluded. On April 12, 2008, the owners of *Le Ponant* paid the ransom. The 30 hostages were released to a

nearby French military vessel, which took them to Djibouti.

French forces, including a warship and helicopters, had been closely monitoring the yacht during this crisis. Once the hostages were safe, French commandos went after the Somali pirates. The president of France, Nicolas Sarkozy, had approved a military operation to chase down and capture the yacht's hijackers.

The pirates left *Le Ponant* with the ransom money. When they reached shore, six of them got into a pickup truck. As they drove away, attack helicopters carrying French troops suddenly swooped down on them, chasing the pirate vehicle inland to the village of Jariban. French snipers fired shots into the engine, which stopped the truck. Two helicopters landed and took the six Somalis into custody. With them was a sack holding their share of the ransom

After the ransom was paid, small military boats picked up the crew of the luxury yacht *Le Ponant* (pictured at left) and took them to safety on a nearby French warship. In the bottom photo, a French navy helicopter intercepts some of the pirates who had held the *Le Ponant* crew hostage.

money, about $200,000. The six Somalis were taken to France, where they would stand trial for piracy.

Before that trial could be held, Somali pirates would strike again. On September 2, 2008, a group of pirates captured the 50-foot-long yacht *Carre d'As IV*, which had been sailing from Australia to France. The pirates demanded a ransom of 1 million euros (about $1.5 million at that time) for the two French citizens who were sailing the yacht, Jean-Yves Delanne and his wife Bernadette. They also demanded the release of the six Somalis captured in the *Le Ponant* incident.

The French government's response was to launch a raid on September 16 to rescue the Delannes. Thirty French commandos parachuted into the sea near the yacht. They swam to the *Carre d'As IV* and overpowered the pirates, freeing the hostages. One pirate was killed and six others were captured. They were taken to France, where they joined the other Somali pirates awaiting trial.

In April 2009, a similar event occurred, but this time the result was not as good. The *Tanit*, a French yacht, was carrying its 28-year-old captain, Florent Lemaçon, his wife Chloe, their three-year-old son Colin, and two other friends, to Kenya when the vessel was captured by pirates. The Somalis were hostile to their French hostages. They threatened to kill them and blow up the ship. Because of this, the French government again ordered French special forces to attempt a rescue. (Interestingly, the *Tanit* hostage rescue attempt occurred at the same time that the U.N. Navy was pondering a similar pirate-hostage situation a few hundred miles away involving the *Maersk Alabama*.)

On April 10, 2009, French commandos approached the *Tanit* in two speedboats. As they stormed the yacht, the French soldiers became involved in a gun battle with the pirates. Two pirates were killed and three others were captured. However, Florent Lemaçon was also killed during the fighting.

French president Sarkozy defended the decision to take military action against Somali pirates. A statement from Sarkozy's office expressed regret for Lemaçon's death, but promised that commando raids to free hostages would continue, emphasizing "France's determination not to give into blackmail, and to defeat the pirates."

In November and December 2009, the Somali pirates who had captured

A French frigate stops a suspicious-looking fishing dhow in the Gulf of Aden during an antipiracy patrol. After the 2008 yacht hijackings, France joined other European Union countries in a joint naval operation dubbed EU NAVFOR Somalia—Atalanta. The mission is to protect ships sailing off the cost of east Africa and to arrest and disarm pirates.

(Left) French sailors interrogate the crew of a *dhow* suspected of being a pirate mothership. EU NAVFOR boarding parties search suspicious ships and remove weapons or smuggled goods, such as drugs. Small skiffs that are likely to be used for pirate attacks, such as the one below, are often destroyed.

the *Carre d'As IV* were tried in Paris. Five of the six were found guilty and sentenced to four to eight years in prison. The sixth man was freed because he was under age 18 when the attack occurred.

In May 2012 the six pirates who had captured *Le Ponant* were tried in Paris. Speaking through interpreters, one of the men admitted to piracy. Two claimed to have been on board the yacht as vendors trying to sell cigarettes and goats. Three denied that they were ever aboard *Le Ponant*. The two youngest Somalis were acquitted, having already spent four years in a French prison. The other four pirates were convicted and sentenced to between four and ten additional years in prison.

Lynn Rival Hijacking
The Chandlers' Ordeal

After they retired, 55-year old Rachel Chandler and 58-year-old Paul Chandler planned to spend their retirement years sailing around the world on their yacht, the 38-foot-long *Lynn Rival*. Instead, in the fall of 2009 the British couple fell victim to Somali pirates, who held them in captivity for more than a year, often under brutal conditions.

By 2009 the Chandlers had been sailing full-time for several years on the *Lynn Rival*. They blogged about their adventures along the Adriatic, the Red Sea, Egypt, India, and Oman. On October 22, 2009, the couple set out from Mahe, a major island of the Seychelles group, en route to Tanga, Tanzania. After a day and a half in the Indian Ocean, they were surprised by pirates boarding their yacht.

Rachel, who was keeping watch while Paul was asleep below deck, did not see or hear their approach in the nighttime darkness. The noise of pirates clambering aboard woke him up, and he quickly set off a distress radio beacon known as the EPIRB. It alerted authorities in the Seychelles that the *Lynn Rival* was in trouble. The Chandlers also sent a distress signal over the internet.

At first, authorities in the Seychelles did not know what to make of the EPIRB signal. The pirates had switched it off soon after boarding the yacht, so they feared the vessel had sunk. They launched a search for the *Lynn Rival*, which was joined by warships from Combined Task Force 151, NATO, and the European Union.

On October 27, 2009, an EU NAVFOR warship reported that it had spotted a yacht towing a skiff about 200 miles to the east of Harardhere, a notorious pirate base in central Somalia. The yacht was soon positively identified as the *Lynn Rival*.

The 38-foot yacht *Lynn Rival* sails in the Indian Ocean. This photo of the hijacked vessel was taken by the helicopter of a Spanish warship while flying an antipiracy patrol.

On the yacht, the pirates held the couple at gunpoint as they ransacked the boat, stealing jewelry, electronics, food, and clothes. The pirates then sailed the ship to Harardhere, where they anchored the yacht. Believing the British couple to be wealthy, the pirates demanded a large ransom of $7 million. But the Chandlers and their families did did not have access to such a large sum.

From England, Rachel's older brother Stephen Collett made hundreds of phone calls, trying to negotiate a lower ransom with the pirates. Complicating matters was the British government's refusal to allow the Chandlers' relatives to access Rachel and Paul's bank accounts, even though the Chandlers were willing to exchange their life savings for their freedom.

Generally, pirates will keep their hostages on the captured vessels while ransom negotiations take place. In this case, however, the pirates forced the Chandlers to go ashore. The two were kept in camps near the village of Amara, a few miles inland from the coast. In these camps in the desert, the hostages were fed a sparse diet of goat meat, rice, and spaghetti.

The kidnapping of the Chandlers was front-page news in Britain, where there is a significant community of Somali exiles. It is believed that between 250,000 and 500,000 Somalis have been living in the United Kingdom since the collapse of their country's government in the early 1990s. Embarrassed by the Chandlers' story, several British Somalis attempted to raise money to help ransom the couple. However, the British government discouraged this because of a policy not to pay ransom to pirates.

As negotiations dragged on, the pirates began to abuse the Chandlers. Both of them were beaten, and they were held separately. For three months, neither one knew whether the other was still alive. They were weakened by the poor treatment and lack of nourishing food.

In January 2010, a Somali doctor visited the Chandlers. When a video made during his visit aired in Britain, people were shocked. The Chandlers looked gaunt and sick. This inspired new efforts to gain the couple's release. The Saleban, one of the major clans in the Amara region, was asked to intervene with the pirates and ask them to set the Chandlers free.

In mid-June 2010, the Chandlers signed an agreement to pay $450,000 for their release. But although the payment was made, the couple remained in captivity. The pirates had decided to hold out for more money.

Ultimately an additional amount of ransom was paid. Details of how much the pirates received, and who actually provided the money, have never been officially released. Some reports indicated that part of the money was donated by Somali exiles in the United Kingdom. Others said that Somalia's TFG government had paid part of the ransom.

On November 13, 2010, the pirates released Rachel and Paul Chandler. They had been held hostage for 388 days. The Chandlers returned to England, where they learned that the *Lynn Rival* had been recovered by the British Navy. They gave interviews about their ordeal and started working on a book, *Hostage*, which was published in 2011.

In September 2012 the British newspaper *The Guardian* reported that the Chandlers were back at sea, planning to continue their travels around the world. "We're comfortable," Rachel Chandler told the newspaper. "We've gone through it, and it was a horrendous experience, but we were very unlucky. We can't pretend it didn't happen; it did. But we know that underneath we are still the same people. And you do have to get on with life."

Somalia's Prime Minister Mohamed Abdullahi Mohamed (center) addresses the media while flanked by released British hostages Rachel and Paul Chandler in Mogadishu, November 14, 2010. The Chandlers were released after more than a year in captivity.

The large container ship Maersk Alabama *was carrying food from humanitarian groups to starving people in East Africa when it was hijacked by pirates in April 2009.*

13

MAERSK ALABAMA
A CAPTAIN'S COURAGE

On April 6, 2009, Somali pirates captured a Taiwanese fishing vessel called *Win Far* 161, which they used as a mothership in attacking other ships. Two days later, on April 8, it supported the attack by four pirates on a 17,000-ton American container ship, MV *Maersk Alabama*, as it traveled off the Somali coast on its way to Mombasa, Kenya. It was the first American merchant ship to be hijacked in 200 years.

The crew of the *Maersk Alabama* had been trained in antipiracy techniques, and they tried to prevent the pirates from boarding their ship. One crew member later explained that they kept swinging the ship's rudder from side to side, which caused the pirate skiff to capsize. Nonetheless, the pirates were able to clamber aboard the *Maersk Alabama*.

Once the pirates were aboard, however, they found that they could not control the ship from the bridge. The crew had shut down the ship's engine, as well as the ship's power, which plunged the areas below deck into darkness. Most of the crew took refuge in a safe room there. When one of the pirates tried to find them, he was taken prisoner.

But the pirates captured the captain of the *Maersk Alabama*, Richard Phillips, who had remained on the bridge. Since their skiff had been lost, Phillips offered the pirates one of the ship's motorized lifeboats if they would leave. The crew agreed to exchange their pirate prisoner for the captain when the pirates took the lifeboat. But the plan went awry. The pirates took the lifeboat and freed their friend, but Phillips remained a captive.

"We were supposed to exchange their guy for the Captain, but they ended up keeping him," a crew member

(Top) The container ship *Maersk Alabama* sails along the Kenyan coast. (Bottom) Frame from a video taken by surveillance aircraft shows the pirate-occupied *Maersk Alabama* in the Indian Ocean during April 2009.

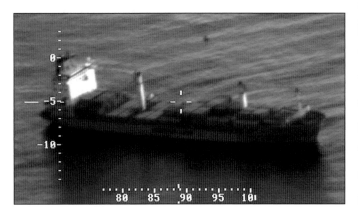

explained later. "They motored off in the lifeboat. They had no way of getting back aboard, so we followed them."

The American navy destroyer USS *Bainbridge* arrived on the scene after Phillips had become a hostage on the 18-foot, covered orange lifeboat. The captain of the *Bainbridge*, Commander Frank Castellano, directed the crew of the *Maersk Alabama* to leave the area and continue on to Mombasa, accompanied by an armed warship. Castellano wanted to get the container ship out of danger, as it was believed other pirates might be coming to support the *Maersk Alabama* hijackers.

Aware that naval warships and helicopters were closing in, the pirates on the *Maersk Alabama* had contacted fellow pirates by satellite phone. One of their leaders onshore was Abdi Garaad, who spoke on the phone with the media and U.S. authorities. He demanded a $2 million payment for his help in ending the standoff. The pirates wanted ransom along with confirmation that they would not be arrested if they released the captain. They threatened to kill Phillips if their demands were not met.

On April 9, the commander of the *Bainbridge* initiated communications with the pirates. He did not discuss the ransom demands. Instead, he insisted that the pirates release Captain Phillips and surrender. The following day, Phillips attempted to escape by jumping into the sea. He tried to swim to the destroyer, but the four pirates jumped in after him, hauled him back into the lifeboat, and tied him up so he could not attempt another escape.

The pirates began running out of food and fuel during the standoff, so a small boat from the *Bainbridge* brought the pirates and their hostage food and water. One of the pirates needed medical treatment for a gash on his hand, so he went back on the boat to the *Bainbridge*. The other three pirates remained with Captain Phillips on the covered lifeboat.

Four days after boarding the *Maersk Alabama*, the pirates agreed to have the lifeboat towed on a 100-foot line by the American destroyer. By this time, a team of U.S. Navy SEALs had come aboard the *Bainbridge*. President Barack Obama had authorized the SEALs, who were trained snipers, to

An American navy team climbs onto the lifeboat of the *Maersk Alabama*, in which Captain Richard Phillips was held hostage by pirates for four days.

Maersk Alabama Captain Richard Phillips (right) stands with Commander Frank Castellano of USS *Bainbridge* after being rescued by the U.S Navy off the coast of Somalia.

rescue Phillips if it appeared that he was in danger of being killed and if they had clear shots.

At around 7:19 P.M. on the evening of April 12, those watching the lifeboat saw that one of the pirates had aimed his AK-47 rifle at Captain Phillips's back. Commander Castellano decided that the captain's life was in danger and told the SEALs to proceed.

On the stern of the *Bainbridge*, the three snipers waited with high-powered rifles equipped with telescopic "night-vision" sights. When two of the pirates poked their heads out of the rear hatch, the three snipers each aimed at a target. They fired simultaneously, killing the three pirates. Captain Phillips, who was unharmed, was quickly rescued from the lifeboat.

The lone pirate survivor, who had been onboard the *Bainbridge* when his associates were killed, was sent back to the United States for trial. Abduwali Muse was around 17 years old when he participated in the attack on the *Maersk Alabama*. At the federal court in New York, he pled guilty and was sentenced to at least 33 years in prison.

Captain Phillips was hailed as a hero after his release. He returned to the United States and met with President Obama at the White House. "I share the country's admiration for the bravery of Captain Phillips and his selfless concern for his crew," commented Obama. "His courage is a model for all Americans." However, months after the incident some members of the *Maersk Alabama*'s crew criticized the captain, saying that he had carelessly ignored several warnings that pirates were operating in the area.

Seven months later, in November 2009, the *Maersk Alabama* was attacked by pirates a second time. This time, the shipping company had stationed armed security guards onboard, and they repelled the pirates using evasive maneuvers, small-arms fire, and a long range acoustic device.

14

PROSECUTING PIRATES

International law regarding piracy can be found in Article 101 of the United Nations Convention on the Law of the Sea (UNCLOS). It states:

Piracy consists of any of the following acts:

(a) any illegal acts of violence or detention, or any act of depredation, committed for private ends by the crew or the passengers of a private ship or a private aircraft, and directed:

(i) on the high seas, against another ship or aircraft, or against persons or property on board such ship or aircraft;

(ii) against a ship, aircraft, persons or property in a place outside the jurisdiction of any State;

(b) any act of voluntary participation in the operation of a ship or of an aircraft with knowledge of facts making it a pirate ship or aircraft;

(c) any act of inciting or of intentionally facilitating an act described in subparagraph (a) or (b).

According to international law, sovereign nations have the right to capture and prosecute pirates arrested on the high seas (that is, in international waters). However, only a few nations have brought Somali pirates to trial. Many governments are deterred from taking legal action due to the expense and difficulty of trying cases far away from where the crime occurred. It can be a challenge to make sure that witnesses and evidence are available when those suspected of piracy are tried.

Another issue is that determining which nation has legal jurisdiction in piracy cases can be complicated. Should such cases be tried by the state in which the vessel is registered, or by the country of the company that owns the ship? Or should jurisdiction depend on the the citizenship of the crew members? If so, this would be complicated by the

Smoke rises from a pirate skiff disabled by an American antipiracy patrol in the Gulf of Aden. Due to the difficulty of prosecuting pirates, warships that encounter suspected pirates but don't have a legal reason to arrest them will take their weapons and disable their ability to launch future attacks.

fact that shipping crews generally include sailors of many nationalities. Or, should cases be tried by the state that owns the warship that arrested the pirates? These questions have never been resolved on an international level.

Over the past decade the navies of some two dozen countries have captured hundreds of Somali pirates. Some of them have been tried for their crimes, or are in prison awaiting trial. However, because of the difficulties in prosecuting pirate trials, many others suspected of pirate activity have simply been detained, disarmed, and set free.

Because there is no effective central government in Somalia capable of asserting sovereign rights or of prosecuting criminals, the pirates seized in international waters are not remanded into Somali custody. For a time Somalis arrested for suspected piracy were taken to Kenya, which borders Somalia to the south. The Kenyan government had signed agreements in 2009 with several Western nations in which it agreed to take accused Somalis into custody and prosecute them for piracy. But a lack of financial support for pirate trials led Kenyan officials to refuse to take on any more pirate cases after April 2010.

In June of that year, an internationally funded UN-supported maritime court was established at Shimo la Tewa prison in Mombasa, Kenya. But a Kenyan judge later ruled that the court did not have legal jurisdiction in piracy cases. As of January 2011 more than 130 men suspected of piracy were being held in Kenya, but had not been brought to trial because of inadequate funding.

In 2010 Seychelles also established a UN-financed piracy court to prosecute suspected pirates seized by foreign navies. A prison facility to hold defendants and convicted pirates was established and funded by the United Nations.

In a few cases, accused pirates have been tried in courts in Abu Dhabi, United Arab Emirates; Amsterdam, the Netherlands; Hamburg, Germany; and Paris. In the United States, pirates have been tried for attacking American ships in federal courts in New York and Norfolk, Virginia.

Yuri Fedotov

"Piracy is immensely damaging to local economies and to local livelihoods," the executive director of the United Nations' Office on Drugs and Crime's piracy program, Yuri Fedotov, noted in November 2012. "In the Seychelles, it has prevented ships from fishing; between Kenya and Uganda it is raising transport costs; and from Somalia, some 1,200 fit and able young men have been detained and imprisoned across the world."

That month the United Nations Security Council renewed international efforts to stop piracy. It called on "all Member States to criminalize piracy under their domestic laws and to assist Somalia in strengthening its capacity to bring to justice those involved in piracy . . . and to cooperate in investigations of all incidents, stressing that all such measures must be consistent with international law."

A French antipiracy patrol arrests Somali pirates in a small boat in the Gulf of Aden.

15

The Quest Hijacking
A Deadly Confrontation

On February 2, 2011, the one Somali pirate who had survived the *Maersk Alabama* incident received a long prison sentence from an American judge. In Somalia, angry pirates told reporters that they would strike back at the United States to avenge their associate. About two weeks later, Somali pirates seized American citizens for the second time when they hijacked a yacht traveling through the Indian Ocean. Like the *Maersk Alabama* attack, this hijacking would also end in violence—only with a tragic ending.

The 58-foot-long yacht *Quest* was owned and operated by Scott and Jean Adam, who had sold their California home to purchase the vessel in 2004. Over the next decade the couple sailed the *Quest* all over the world. For several months of each year, they would anchor at Marina Del Rey, California. The rest of the time they spent traveling to exotic locations, such as New Zealand, South America, China, Thailand, and India. Along the way, the Adams liked to distribute bibles to Christian churches in the regions they visited.

In February 2011 the Adams were traveling around the world with two other Americans, Phyllis Macay and Robert Riggle, who were from Seattle, Washington.

Until February 15, 2011, the *Quest* had been sailing with a rally—a convoy of yachts and small vessels that travel together in order to ward off pirate attacks. But after stopping at Mumbai, India, the *Quest* left the group in order to take an alternate route to Salalah, Oman. Three days later the yacht was traveling alone outside designated shipping lanes, about 275 miles from the coast of Oman, when Somali pirates attacked and boarded the *Quest*.

When the pirates attacked, someone on the *Quest* sent out a distress signal. Warships from the U.S. Navy's Fifth Fleet responded quickly to the distress call. When the warships arrived, troops observed a pirate mothership near the yacht, but this vessel sped away. The Americans soon learned that the mothership had ferried 19 pirate gunmen to the small yacht. The swift appearance of the naval patrol prevented the pirates from transferring their four hostages to the much faster and well-stocked mothership. The pirates planned to take the yacht and hostages back to Somalia.

Over the next few days, as the pirates steered the *Quest* toward Somali waters, it was closely shadowed by the guided-missile destroyer USS *Sterett*. Three other Navy warships—the aircraft carrier USS *Enterprise*, the cruiser USS *Leyte Gulf*, and the destroyer USS *Bulkeley*—remained nearby, while military helicopters hovered overhead.

Tensions were running high when two of the pirates went aboard the *Sterett* on February 21 to discuss the release of the hostages. But no agreement was reached, and the pirates were detained aboard the warship. Navy officials also negotiated by phone with the pirates' leader, as well as with Somali village elders in Hobyo, where the yacht was headed.

At around 1 A.M. on February 22, 2011, one of the pirates on the *Quest*

Scott and Jean Adam were experienced sailors. They tried to use their radio sparingly while traveling alone to Oman across the Indian Ocean, so that they couldn't be tracked by pirates, but their vessel was found and captured nonetheless.

fired a rocket-propelled grenade at the *Sterett*. Gunfire then erupted inside the yacht's cabin, where the hostages were being held. Immediately 15 Navy SEALs rushed to the yacht, where they killed two pirates. When the shooting stopped, the SEALs found the bodies of two other pirates, who had been killed

Jean Adam kept track of the *Quest*'s journeys on this website, www.svquest.com.

The USS *Sterett's* VBSS team leaves the warship and approaches the pirate-controlled vessel.

earlier, as well as the four Americans. It appeared that the Somali pirates had disagreed about something, and the pirates and hostages had been killed.

However, other pirates in Somali claimed that all the deaths occurred after U.S. forces launched a rescue attempt. "When Americans tried to rescue the hostages and arrest our friends, our friends decided to fight until death," Somali pirate Ali Jama told *Time* magazine. "The U.S. navy forces started the shootings. They are to be blamed for what happened."

U.S. forces arrested the 13 remaining pirates aboard the ship, along with the two who were detained on the *Sterett*. They also went after the man who had served as the ransom negotiator, Mohammad Saaili Shibin. He was arrested by the FBI in Somalia and brought to the United States to face trial in Norfolk, Virginia, for his role in the deaths of the four Americans. Convicted of 15 charges, including piracy, kidnapping, and hostage-taking, he was sentenced to 12 life sentences and ordered to pay $5.4 million in restitution.

The other pirates were also tried in Norfolk. As of August 2012 eleven of the 15 surviving pirates aboard the *Quest* had pled guilty and been sentenced to life in prison. One was released because he is a juvenile. Three others, who were charged with shooting the Americans, face the death penalty.

16

SIRIUS STAR
THE FIRST HIJACKED SUPERTANKER

L ess than two months after Somali pirates frightened the world with their hijacking of the weapons-laden *Faina*, another group of pirates seized an oil supertanker. The capture of the Liberian-flagged *Sirius Star* on November 15, 2008, shocked observers for several reasons. It was the first time that pirates had taken control of an oil supertanker, and it was the biggest ship ever captured by pirates. The double-hulled 162,252-ton oil tanker was 1,080 feet long and almost 200 feet wide. At three times the mass of a U.S. aircraft carrier, it was considered too large to be hijacked.

Of even greater concern was that this was the first time Somali pirates had struck so far out to sea. The *Sirius Star* had been traveling hundreds of miles away from the coast of east Africa, at about twice the distance considered to be safe from pirates. At that

time in 2008 the International Maritime Bureau had set guidelines advising ships to travel at least 250 miles from the coast. But the pirate gang had captured a Nigerian tugboat that they were using as a mothership, and this enabled them to launch their attack much farther from shore. When the pirates attacked the *Sirius Star* it was 520 miles southeast of Mombasa, Kenya.

The *Sirius Star*, a VLCC owned by Vela International, a Dubai-based subsidiary of the national oil company of Saudi Arabia, was carrying a load of crude oil worth about $100 million. The ship's scheduled route was to travel south along the coast of Africa, round the Cape of Good Hope, then sail north to the Caribbean to deliver its cargo. The *Sirius Star* carried a crew of 25 sailors, who were of many different nationalities: British, Croatian, Filipino, Polish, and Saudi.

Pirate skiffs tied up at the stern of the supertanker *Sirius Star*.

When *Sirius Star* captain Marek Niski realized that pirate skiffs were approaching his ship, he increased the enormous vessel's speed and ordered crew members to use the fire hoses to repel the pirates. But two fiberglass speedboats, carrying eight armed pirates, caught up with the tanker. As pirates fired warning shots with their AK-47 assault rifles and rocket-propelled grenades, the captain told members of the crew to find safety below the *Sirius Star*'s deck.

The sea bandits tossed a rope ladder with a grappling hook over the stern guardrail. They clambered up to the ship's deck and stormed the bridge. After taking control of the *Sirius Star*, they steered it to meet up with their mothership, which carried 10 more pirates who reinforced the original attackers. The pirates rounded up the crew members and held them hostage in the ship.

Although warships from the U.S. Navy's Fifth Fleet soon caught up to the

Sirius Star, the military found itself unable to do anything. If marines or commandos tried to storm the ship, the hostages could be killed. Of greater concern was the danger that the ship could be damaged or sunk, venting some 2 million barrels of crude oil into the sea and causing an environmental catastrophe.

Having gained full control over their prize, the pirates confidently set course for Somalia. Two days later they were joined by 25 more pirates. The *Sirius Star* was anchored off the coast of northeastern Somalia near the pirate haven town of Harardhere.

On November 18, pirate intermediaries contacted the supertanker's own-ers and demanded a $25 million ransom for the *Sirius Star* and its crew, to be paid within 10 days. One pirate spokesman warned that if these demands were not met, the consequences would be "disastrous." The Al-Jazeera news network, which airs in Arab countries, broadcast an audiotape said to be from the pirate group in which a man demanded that the ransom be delivered to the ship in cash, where he claimed it would be mechanically counted. He also stated that the pirates had the technology to determine whether any of the bills received were counterfeit.

Five more weeks would pass before a ransom price of $3 million was agreed

The hijacked *Sirius Star* at anchor off the coast of Harardhere a notorious pirate haven.

Ransom is dropped by parachute onto the deck of the *Sirius Star*, January 9, 2009.

upon. On the morning of January 9, 2009, the pirates agreed to show authorities that the hostages were okay. Members of the crew were brought up on deck while a plane flew overhead to see that they were unharmed. After this, a package containing half the promised ransom, $1.5 million in cash, was dropped by parachute onto the deck of the *Sirius Star*. Later the same day, the second half of the payment was dropped onboard.

Pirates on the ship eagerly counted and divided up the money. Celebrating their shares of newfound wealth, more than a dozen of them set off from the ship in small dinghies. Five of the pirates never made it to shore with their loot, however—they drowned when their boat capsized. The following day, January 10, 2009, the final 18 pirates aboard the *Sirius Star* freed the crew and left the ship.

SOMALIA
A HAVEN FOR MODERN PIRATES

Somalia has had no effective central government since May 1991, when the government headed by Mohamed Siad Barre was overthrown. Since then, Somalia's 8 million people have struggled with violence, severe poverty, and lawlessness. Somalis speak a common language (Somali) and most follow the same religion (Sunni Islam). However, the people of Somalia are divided by clan allegiance. Since the fall of the Barre regime, fighting between clans and factions has gone on for more than two decades.

In October 2004 a Transitional Federal Government (TFG) was formed with the help of the United Nations. Supported by the United States, the TFG holds only limited control in Somalia (basically, it controls just the area around the capital city, Mogadishu). The Somali TFG has been opposed since 2006 by an Islamist insurgent group, al-Shabaab. Violence by al-Shabaab militants has kept Somalia in turmoil. The Transitional Federal Government has also been challenged by the emergence of numerous clan-based local governments, as well as two semi-autonomous areas within Somalia that have declared their independence—Somaliland, established in 1991, and Puntland, in 1998.

The problem of Somali pirates today is a direct result of the collapse of Somalia's government in the early 1990s. The lack of an effective central governing authority left Somalia's 1,880-mile-long coastline unprotected. The waters off the coast were targeted by foreign fishermen, who could use methods that produced large catches of fish but were very destructive to the marine environment. This included blast fishing, in which dynamite was detonated to stun or kill large schools of

Somalia is one of the world's poorest countries, and its people have suffered from war and famine since the early 1990s. These people are waiting for food at a refugee camp in southern Somalia. By 2011, the U.N. estimated that nearly half of the country's population was in crisis and in urgent need of assistance.

fish. Blast fishing destroys coral reefs, and is illegal in most places, but with no one to enforce the laws fishermen could do whatever they wanted. Foreign fishing trawlers destroyed marine floors by using drag-fishing nets to scoop up tuna, shark, lobster, and shrimp. Foreign companies also dumped toxic chemicals into the water.

These practices made it harder for poor Somalis who lived near the ocean to make a living from fishing. In response, Somali fisherman armed themselves and began to attack the for-

eign vessels. They would forcibly board fishing boats and demanding payment of "fines," that could be several thousand dollars. The Somali vigilante groups did not consider themselves pirates. Instead, the referred to themselves as defenders of Somalia's territorial waters, calling themselves by names like the "Central Somali Coast Guard," and "Ocean Salvation Corps."

Some of the Somali fishermen eventually moved on to stopping and ransoming commercial ships. They claimed they were not only confronting trawlers engaged in illegal fishing but also foreign ships dumping poisonous waste in Somali waters.

By 2008 Somali piracy had developed into a ransom-driven business. The groups are highly organized with investors, accountants, and a pirate leader working on land, and the attack groups, or militia, working at sea. The members of a pirate group typically belong to the same local clan.

Members of pirate militias are taught how to use machine guns like the AK-47 rifle, rocket-propelled grenades, and anti-tank missiles. Some pirates are young men who know how to use speedboats equipped with satellite phones and global positioning system equipment. Others are trained for particular jobs once the group is on board a hijacked ship, such as navigating the vessel or operating equipment.

The members of pirate crews are often paid by the leaders in advance. This money comes from "investors"— wealthy Somalis who finance pirate raids as an investment, with the expectation that they will get a large share of any profits or ransom payment. In addition to paying for weapons and to outfit pirate skiffs, upfront money is used to keep hostages fed and sheltered while negotiations with ship owners or the hostages' families are underway. The pirate leaders also must provide food and supplies to hostage guards. The pirates often require an ongoing supply of *khat*, a narcotic-like leaf that Somalis chew to provide a mild high. Additional expenses may include paying money for translators and ransom negotiators.

One of the key causes of Somali piracy is poverty. Hijacking ships for ransom brings money and jobs into the

Members of the U.N. Security Council unanimously adopt a resolution condemning all acts of piracy and armed robbery against vessels off the coast of Somalia, and authorizing measures to combat piracy, in June 2008.

Peacekeeping troops from the African Union capture weapons used by the Islamist group al-Shabaab, which has been fighting against the Somali Transitional Federal Government. The civil war in Somalia has weakened the government's ability to deal with pirates. Pirates have been known to pay al-Shabaab when the group allows them to operate in areas controlled by the Islamists.

impoverished towns that serve as pirate bases. The most infamous pirate havens in Somalia include the towns of Caluula, Eyl, Garacad, Harardhere (also spelled Xarardheere), and Hobyo. Pirates prepare for and launch their raids from these towns, and return with captured vessels and hostages. Townspeople are hired to work as guards, cooks, deckhands, mechanics, and skiff builders. They provide food and supplies to militias onshore and to hostage vessels anchored offshore. The communities are generally supportive of pirates because the "pirate economy" supports the townspeople. People in many coastal villages regard piracy as legal and consider pirates to be folk heroes.

Efforts to reduce piracy by stabilizing the Somali Transitional Federal Government led the UN in 2009 to pro-vide more than $250 million for African Union peacekeeping forces, as well as other measures intended to strengthen the government and improve the lives of law-abiding Somalis. However, until the Somali TFG can assert its control over the country by enforcing laws and policing the coastline, piracy will remain a problem.

The use of international naval patrols in the Gulf of Aden, as well as armed guards and other security measures on merchant ships, have reduced the number of attacks by Somali pirates. From January to November 2012 there were 71 attempted ship boardings, compared to 199 attempts during same period in 2011. Only 13 ships were hijacked in 2012, compared to 49 in 2010 and 28 in 2011. In October 2012 the IMB reported that Somali piracy was at a three year low.

SOMALI PIRATE LEADERS

Three of the most notorious pirate leaders in Somalia responsible for the hijackings of hundreds of ships include Abdullahi Abshir Boyah, Mohamed Abdi Hassan, and Mohamed Abdi Garaad.

Sometimes referred to as the "pioneer pirate," Abdullahi Abshir Boyah is a member of the Majerteen, a subclan of the Darood clan in Somalia. As an adult he worked as a lobster fisherman, and was among the first Somali fishermen to participate in hijacking foreign trawlers that were fishing illegally off the coast in the early 1990s. Boyah soon moved on to hijacking commercial shipping vessels. By the 2000s Boyah was a full-time pirate leader, acting as organizer, recruiter, financier, and mission commander. His hometown of Eyl became a pirate capital.

Over a 10-year period, Boyah and his pirate gangs have hijacked at least 30 ships. They are believed to have carried out one of the first hijackings of a major commercial ship in the Gulf of Aden. In October 2007 Boyah and his gang seized the Japanese chemical tanker *Golden Nori*. The USS *Porter*

A boarding team from a U.S. Navy warship approaches the merchant vessel *Golden Nori* after pirates led by Abdullahi Boyah released the Japanese chemical tanker, December 12, 2007.

Some merchant ships have begun winding barbed wire around the stern and gunwales. This makes it more difficult for pirates to board the vessel.

Ponant, which brought the gang roughly $1.8 million in ransom; French special forces captured six pirates and recovered about $200,000 of the original $2 million ransom.

In April 2010 the U.S. Treasury Department, which had been given the power to freeze the assets of individuals involved in piracy off Somalia's coast, froze Boyah's accounts. The following month, in a crackdown on pirates operating in the area, the government of Puntland arrested Boyah. He was sentenced to eight years in prison and is currently serving time in a U.N.-built jail in Bosaso, Puntland. In an interview the pirate explained that he had been arrested because "I took one ship too many."

Mohamed Abdi Hassan, nicknamed *Afweyne* ("Big Mouth") was a former Somali government employee who had no money when he arrived in Puntland in 2003. Afweyne soon built a pirate operation in the coastal town of Harardhere. As a pirate boss he became extremely wealthy, funneling ransom money back into the training and arming of one of the largest Somali pirate gangs, a militia he called the Somali Marines. Afweyne served as head of financial operations and never went to sea. He treated piracy as a business, bringing in investors to finance pirate missions and working with other pirate groups. He is a member of the Habir Gedir, a subclan of the Hawiye, which is

quickly responded and destroyed the pirates' two skiffs, stranding the pirates onboard. But because the tanker contained volatile chemicals, the warship did not fire on it. Eventually the pirate chief obtained not only safe passage off the ship but also a hefty ransom of $1.5 million. Boyah's militia was also behind the hijacking of the French yacht *Le* hostile to the Darood clan to which Boyah and Garaad belong. However, Afweyne set clan rivalries aside to work with the other pirate leaders many times in joint operations.

From 2005 to 2007, Afweyne's pirate militia attacked five vessels carrying supplies from the U.N.'s World Food Programme to Somalia. They successfully hijacked two ships. One was the freighter *Semlow,* a small UN-chartered vessel from Kenya carrying 850 tons of rice that had been donated to tsunami survivors in Somalia. The pirates demanded a ransom of half a million dollars. Negotiations took several months until an agreement was reached in October. Afweyne's group ultimately collected $135,000 in ransom money.

Afweyne accumulated great wealth and influence in Africa. In 2009 he and his son Abidqaadir ransomed seven ships and held them hostage in the towns of Harardhere and Hobyo. That year he was also invited in as a dignitary to celebrations in Tripoli of Muammar al-Gaddafi's 40 years in power in Libya.

As of July 2012 Afweyne was reported to have renounced pirate ways. According to a story in the website *Somalia Report,* he agreed to head the Somali Transitional Federal Government's antipiracy operations in Harardhere, Hobyo, and Southern Somalia.

A former member of Afweyne's gang, Mohamed Abdi Garaad, has continued to operate as a pirate. A native of Eyl and a member of the Darood clan, Garaad formed a pirate militia called the National Volunteer Coast Guard. It operates out of the southern port of Kismaayo. A major organizer and financier of pirate missions, Garaad boasted in 2009 of controlling an organization comprised of 800 pirates, organized into 13 groups.

Garaad's group is responsible for many pirate attacks, including the July 2008 hijacking of the Japanese freighter *Stella Maris* and the April 2009 hijacking of the *Maersk Alabama.* Shortly after three of his men were killed during that operation, Garaad vowed revenge. When his men spotted the U.S.-flagged cargo ship *Liberty Sun* heading for the Kenyan port of Mombasa with international food aid, they attacked. The Somali pirates bombarded the ship with rocket-propelled grenades and automatic weapons. Neither the crew nor ship was harmed. Garaad later told a French news agency, "We were not after a ransom. We . . . assigned a team with special equipment to chase and destroy any ship flying the American flag in retaliation for the brutal killing of our friends."

Sailors man the .50 caliber machine gun on the bow of their warship during an antipiracy patrol in the Straits of Malacca.

SOUTHEAST ASIA AND PIRACY

During the 1990s and early 2000s, more than half of the pirate attacks reported in the world occurred in the waterways of Southeast Asia. The majority of incidents took place in Indonesia's waters and ports.

The piracy around Indonesia was caused in part by political instability in the territory of Aceh, located on the far western edge of the Indonesian island of Sumatra. An Islamic separatist group, the Free Aceh Movement (GAM), had been battling the Indonesian military since the 1970s. In this war-torn region, thousands of people had no money and no work. Piracy had become a way to earn a living. Indonesian fishing boats were easy targets for pirate gangs that extorted payments from fishermen for protection. Boats operating off the coasts of Aceh and North Sumatra were especially vulnerable.

Violence was common. In 1998, 67 sailors were killed in pirate attacks. All but one of those murders occurred in the Straits of Malacca or the South China Sea.

Twenty-three crewmen were killed during one attack in November 1998. They were aboard the Panamanian-flagged merchant vessel *Cheung Son* when it left Shanghai with a cargo of furnace slag, a metallic powder used to produce industrial concrete. The *Cheung Son* was bound for Port Kelang, Malaysia, but it never arrived. Eventually, investigators determined that the entire crew had been brutally murdered by a pirate gang operating in the South China Sea. The pirates probably sold both the cargo and the freighter, as neither have ever been found. However, Chinese police eventually arrested 13 pirates; they were found guilty and executed.

Until the late 1990s, most pirate attacks in Southeast Asia were simple affairs in which ships were boarded and sailors were robbed of cash and valuables. But eventually pirates began stealing entire ships, often setting their crews adrift in lifeboats or killing them. The pirates repainted the vessels, creating phantom ships.

In September 1998 the Japanese freighter *Tenyu* left Kuala Tanjong on the Indonesian island of Sumatra bound for Inchon, South Korea. The ship was located the following December in China. It had been renamed and freshly painted. The *Tenyu*'s cargo (about 3,000 tons of aluminum ingots, worth approximately $6 million) was gone, and its 14-man crew was never found.

In another incident, on June 8, 1999, the Thai tanker *Siam Xanxai* was hijacked. Its 17 crew members had been set adrift, but were rescued. The vessel was found nine days later in the port of Shantou, China.

Four months after this incident, the *Alondra Rainbow* went missing, although this vessel was recovered by the Indian navy while it still contained half its cargo. Another Japanese vessel turned into a phantom ship was the *Global Mars*, which was hijacked in February 2000 off the coast of Thailand during a journey from Malaysia to Haldia, India. Its crew was rescued in Thailand, and the vessel was found in

Zhuhai, China, the following August.

Around this time pirates in southeast Asia also turned to kidnapping sailors for ransom. One of the first reported incidents in Southeast Asia was the June 2001 seizure of the *Tirla Niaga IV*. This ship was anchored off the west coast of Aceh for engine repairs when it was boarded by pirates who stole cash and valuables. When they left, they took the ship's master and second officer with them. The second officer was released within a few days, after a ransom was paid. However, the ship's master was held for six months until the pirates received a ransom of $30,000.

In 2004, even as the number of pirate attacks was rapidly rising all over the world, Southeast Asia continued to account for more than half of the reported attacks (169 that year). The International Maritime Bureau issued a report accusing five major criminal syndicates of being behind the hijackings of large ships taking place in the Straits of Malacca. As these groups continued to target million-dollar ships carrying million-dollar cargos the London-based insurance companies designated the straits in 2005 as a "high-risk" area.

Today, however, the Straits of Malacca and the Singapore Straits are no longer considered among the most dangerous places for ships. This is due, in large part, to the intervention of naval

Armed pirates guard the crew of the Chinese fishing vessel *Tian Yu*, which was captured in the Indian Ocean in November 2008.

forces from Indonesia, Malaysia, Singapore, and Thailand. They work together to aggressively patrol the area as part of the Malacca Straits Patrols, which was created in 2004. Another factor contributing to the decrease in pirate attacks around Indonesia is the political stability that resulting from a peace accord, signed in 2005, that ended the conflict in Aceh.

Still, piracy remains a serious problem in some areas of Southeast Asia, especially for ships at anchor off major seaports. The waters of Bangladesh are considered high risk, especially around port town of Chittagong, the nation's second-largest city. Ships are also at high risk while at anchor in Kochi, a major port city on the west coast of India. There are also reports of piracy in the waters off many of Indonesia's islands, including the Anambas, Natuna Mangkai islands, which lie in the South China Sea.

CHAPTER NOTES

p. 7: "An act of boarding . . ." Graham Gerard Ong-Webb, *Piracy, Maritime Terrorism and Securing the Malacca Straits* (Leiden, the Netherlands: International Institute for Asian Studies, 2006), p. 2.

p. 15: "war risk," One Earth Future Foundation, *Economic Cost of Somali Piracy, 2011*, p. 14. http://oceansbeyondpiracy.org/sites/default/files/economic_cost_of_piracy_2011.pdf

p. 17: "The Kuala Lumpur center . . ." Michael Richardson, "Challenging Marauders' Spread, Navy Recovers a Hijacked Ship: India and China Set Sights on Piracy," *New York Times* (November 23, 1999). http://www.nytimes.com/1999/11/23/news/23iht-pirates.2.t.html

p. 27: "International standards or regimes . . ." Peter Griffiths, "Pirate Guards Need Global Guidelines: U.N. Agency," Reuters (May 17, 2012). http://www.reuters.com/article/2012/05/17/britain-piracy-idUSL5E8GHAE420120517

p. 29: "hostage hell," Debbie Calitz, *Twenty Months in Hostage Hell* (New York: Penguin, 2012), p. 1.

p. 35: "A tanker could be set on fire . . ." Lee Glendinning and James Sturcke, "Pirates Take Over Oil Tanker with British Crew on Board," *The Guardian* (November 17, 2008). http://www.guardian.co.uk/world/2008/nov/17/oil-tanker-pirates

p. 39: "We don't consider . . ." Jeffrey Gettleman, "Q&A with a Pirate: 'We Just Want the Money,'" *New York Times* (September 30, 2008). http://thelede.blogs.nytimes.com/2008/09/30/q-a-with-a-pirate-we-just-want-the-money/

p. 40: "The last warning . . ." Richard Norton-Taylor and Tom Parfitt, "British Commandos Kill Two Pirates in Stand-Off," *The Guardian* (November 12, 2008). http://www.guardian.co.uk/world/2008/nov/13/pirates-killed-gulf-aden

p. 45: "Before Operation Prosperity . . ." Will Ross, "Surviving the Pirates Off the Coast of Nigeria," BBC News (September 11, 2012). http://www.bbc.co.uk/news/world-africa-19555334

p. 49: "If they try again . . ." Abdi Guled, Associated Press, "Somali Pirate Captors Move U.S. Hostage After SEAL Raid," *Christian Science Monitor* (January 27, 2012). http://www.csmonitor.com/World/Latest-News-Wires/2012/0127/Somali-pirate-captors-move-US-hostage-after-SEAL-raid

p. 55: "France's determination not . . ." Xan Rice and Lizzy Davies, "Hostage Killed as French Storm Yacht Held by Somali Pirates," *The Guardian* (April 10, 2009). http://www.guardian.co.uk/world/2009/apr/10/hostage-killed-as-french-storm-pirate-yacht

p. 59: "We're comfortable. We've gone through it . . ." Jon Henley, "The Hijack Couple are Back at Sea—Just Don't Mention the Pirates," *The Guardian* (September 10, 2012). http://www.guardian.co.uk/uk/shortcuts/2012/sep/10/hijack-couple-back-at-sea

p. 61: "We were supposed to . . ." Crewman's e-mail Gives Harrowing Details of Hijacking," CNN (April 20, 2009). http://www.cnn.com/2009/WORLD/africa/04/16/somalia.hijacked.ship.email/index.html

p. 64: "I share the country's admiration . . ." Barack Obama, "Statement by the President on the Rescue of Captain Phillips," White Hosue Office of the Press Secretary (April 12, 2009). http://www.whitehouse.gov/the_press_office/Statement-by-the-President-on-the-Rescue-of-Captain-Phillips/

p. 65: "Piracy consists of . . ." preamble to the United Nations Convention on the Law of the Sea, Part VII: High Seas. Available at http://www.un.org/Depts/los/convention_agreements/texts/unclos/part7.htm

p. 67: "Piracy is immensely . . ." United Nations News Center, "UN Deputy Secretary-General Flags Need for 'Multi-Dimensional' Approach to Combating Piracy," (November 19, 2012). http://www.un.org/apps/news/story.asp?NewsID=43538#.UM94ro58ukI

p 67: "all Member States to criminalize . . ." United Nations News Center, "Unremitting Piracy Off Somalia's Coast Prompts Security Council to Renew 'Authorizations' for International Action for Another Year," (November 21, 2012). http://www.un.org/News/Press/docs/2012/sc10824.doc.htm

p. 70: "When Americans tried to rescue . . ." Nick Wadhams, "American Hostage Deaths: A Case of Pirate Anxiety," *Time* (February 23, 2011). http://www.time.com/time/world/article/0,8599,2053344,00.html

p. 73: "disastrous." Xan Rice and Matthew Weaver, "*Sirius Star* Pirates Demand $25m Ransom," *The Guardian* (November 20, 2008). http://www.guardian.co.uk/world/2008/nov/20/piracy-somalia

p. 80: "I took one ship . . ." Andrew Rosthorn, "UN Fury as the Big Mouth Pirate Talks Peace," New Security Learning. http://www.newsecuritylearning.com/index.php/feature/157-un-fury-as-the-big-mouth-pirate-talks-peace

p. 81: "We were not after . . ." Mohamed Abdi Garaad, quoted in Bahadur, *The Pirates of Somalia*, p. 79.

GLOSSARY

AK-47—a type of assault rifle, a weapon typically used by armies and para-military forces that can be fired either as a fully automatic machine gun or in bursts of three rounds. Originally developed in the Soviet Union during the 1940s, the AK-47 remains the world's most popular assault rifle because it is inexpensive, durable, and easy to use and maintain.

dhow—an ship of Arabic design with a high-swept bow; this type of ship has been used for centuries throughout the Indian Ocean for coastal trading.

International Maritime Bureau (IMB)—a division of the International Chamber Of Commerce that was established in 1981 to fight against all types of maritime crime, including piracy, as well as shipping insurance fraud and other threats to trade. The IMB provides information about new criminal methods and trends to ship owners, so that they can reduce their vulnerability. The organization also runs the IMB Piracy Reporting Centre in Kuala Lumpur, Malaysia, which maintains a 24-hour watch on the world's shipping lanes, reports pirate attacks to local law enforcement agencies, and issues warnings about piracy hotspots to ship owners.

international waters—the seas and oceans outside a sovereign nation's territorial waters; sometimes called the "high seas."

khat—a flowering plant found in East Africa and the Arabian Peninsula. Khat leaves contain a stimulant, similar to amphetamine, that produces a mild high when chewed. In countries like Djibouti, Ethiopia, Somalia, and Yemen, khat is among the most commonly used drugs.

maritime—of or having to do with the ocean or sea.

mothership—a large vessel used by modern pirates as a floating base for operations. The mothership is large enough to carry extra supplies, food, and people and powerful enough to tow smaller skiffs used in pirate raids.

MV—motor vessel or merchant vessel.

nautical mile—a unit of length measured at sea. According to international agreement, a nautical mile is 1,852 metres (6,076 feet) in length, making it slightly longer than a land mile (1,609 meters / 5,280 feet).

phantom ship—an unregistered merchant ship, typically one that has been given a new name and identity by hijackers so that it can be used for criminal purposes, such as smuggling or as a pirate mothership.

rocket-propelled grenade (RPG)—a shoulder-fired weapon that fires rockets equipped with an explosive warhead. The weapon has a relatively short range of about 300 to 500 meters.

safe room—a secure area inside a ship, sometimes called the citadel, where crew members can be protected from pirates who have boarded the ship and are trying to capture or kill the crew. Safe rooms are usually stocked with food and drinks, medical equipment, a satellite phone for contact with the outside world, and other supplies.

skiff—a shallow, flat-bottomed open speedboat often used by modern pirates for raids. Skiffs are much faster and more maneuverable than merchant vessels, enabling the pirates to pull up next to those vessels and board them.

strait—a narrow passageway of water that connects two larger areas of water.

territorial waters—the sea and ocean waters under the jurisdiction of a sovereign state. The UN Convention on the Law of the Sea defines the maximum extent of a nation's territorial waters as 12 nautical miles (about 14 miles) off that nation's coastline.

VLCC—a very large crude oil carrier, sometimes called a "supertanker." VLCCs can carry between 200,000 and 320,000 deadweight tons of petroleum—the equivalent of more than 2 million barrels of oil.

FURTHER READING

Bahadur, Jay. *The Pirates of Somalia: Inside Their Hidden World.* New York: Pantheon Books, 2011.

Chandler, Paul. *Hostage: A Year at Gunpoint with Somali Gangsters.* Edinburgh, UK: Mainstream Publishing, 2011.

Eichstaedt, Peter. *Pirate State: Inside Somalia's Terrorism at Sea.* Chicago: Chicago Review Press, 2010.

McKnight, Terry. *Pirate Alley: Commanding Task Force 151 Off Somalia.* Annapolis, Md.: Naval Institute Press, 2012.

Murphy, Martin. *Somalia: The New Barbary? Piracy and Islam in the Horn of Africa.* New York: Columbia University Press, 2011.

Young, Adam J. *Contemporary Maritime Piracy in Southeast Asia: History, Causes and Remedies.* Leiden, the Netherlands: International Institute for Asian Studies, 2007.

INTERNET RESOURCES

http://combinedmaritimeforces.com/

The website for the U.S.-led multi-national naval partnership Combined Maritime Forces, provides links to its three task forces working to provide maritime security and counter-piracy efforts (CTF-150, CTF-151, and CTF-152).

www.eunavfor.eu

Up-to-date information and statistics on missions, the maritime security center MSCHOA, and other efforts in fighting Somali pirates can be found on the European Union NAVFOR site.

www.icc-ccs.org/piracy-reporting-centre

The International Maritime Bureau's Piracy Reporting Center provides up-to-date information on incidents occurring around the world, and includes links to "piracy news and figures" and "piracy prone areas and warnings."

www.oceansbeyondpiracy.org

Oceans Beyond Piracy is a project of the One Earth Future Foundation, a nonprofit organization that works to combat maritime piracy. It publishes annual studies on the economic and human costs of piracy in Somalia.

www.oni.navy.mil/Intelligence_Community/piracy.htm

This website of the Office of Naval Intelligence features links to the most recent issues of the publications "Piracy Analysis and Warning Weekly" and "World Wide Threat to Shipping."

INDEX

Numbers in **bold italics** refer to captions.

93

About the Author: LeeAnne Gelletly is a freelance author living outside Washington, D.C. She had written several books for young people on geography, history and government, including *Somalia*, *The Kurds*, and *Ecological Issues in Africa*.

Photo Credits: © Crown 2008 (U.K. Ministry of Defence): 24; Danish Refugee Council: 49; Del Rey Yacht Club: 69 (top left; EFE / Elyas Ahmed: 29; EFE / Sarah Elliott: 61; EFE / Luca Zennaro: 33; © 2013 European Union: 2 (bottom); EU NAVFOR Public Affairs Office: 37, 55, 56, 58, 67 (bottom); AFP / Getty Images: 6; © Indian Coast Guard, Ministry of Defence, Government of India: 17; Reuters / Landov: 59; © 2012 Ministère de la Défense (France): 54; © 2013 OTTN Publishing: 8, 9, 43; U.S. Navy Photo: 2 (top), 10, 11, 12, 13, 14, 18, 21, 22, 23, 27, 32, 39, 40, 41, 45, 48, 51, 62, 63, 64, 66, 70, 72, 73, 74, 79, 82, 85, 92, all cover images; used under license from Shutterstock, Inc.: 34, 36, 44, 80; Yuriy Korchagin / Shutterstock.com: 30; www.svquest.com: 69 (top right; bottom); United Nations Photo: 67 (top), 76, 77, 78; Wikimedia Commons: 46.